Colorblind Vision
selected photo essay

"Being colorblind gives an advantage when composing black & white... less confusion"

This special collection of custom quality fine art work exhibits the lonely freedom of a hidden perspective selected from thousands of captures during years of travels. All images presented genuine without edits.

info@BEACHNOISE.com

Joseph Fleming

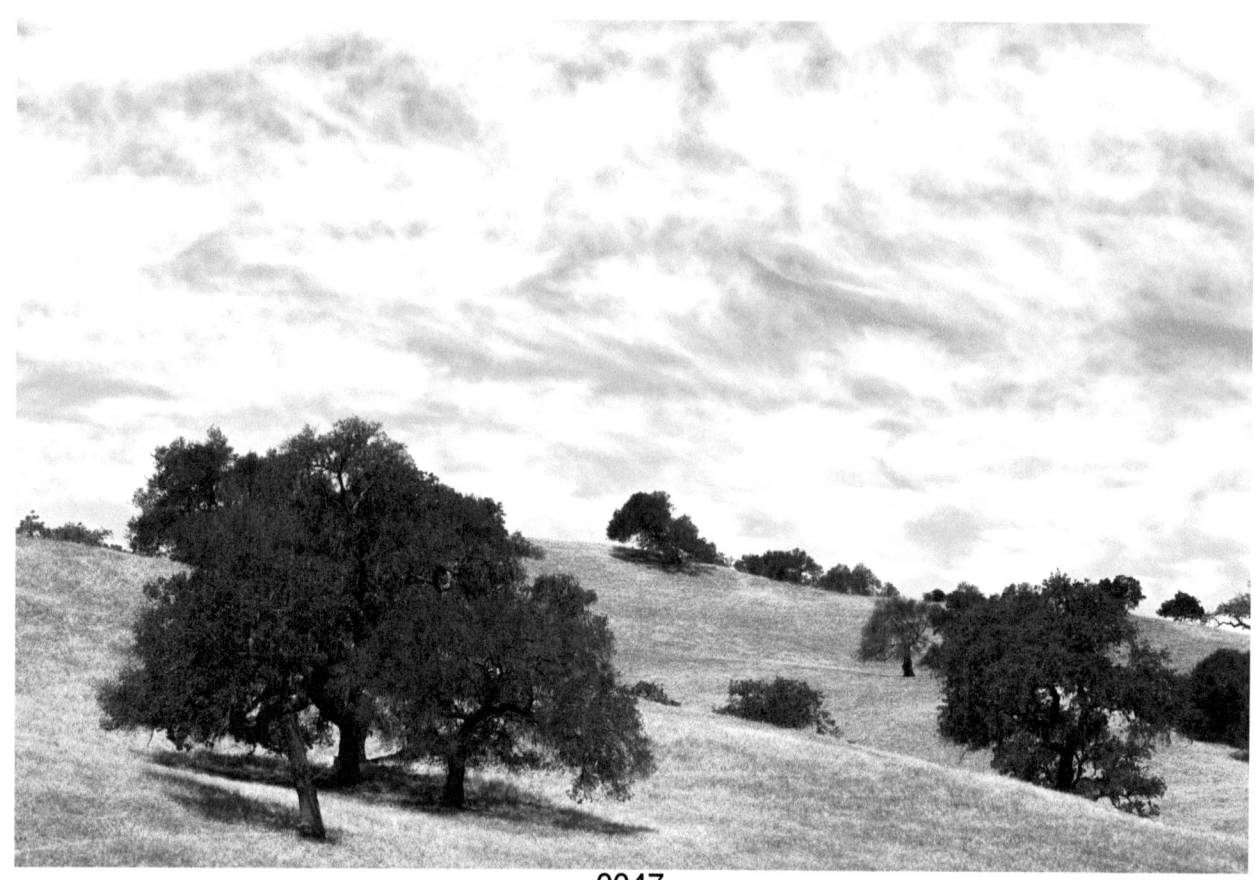

0047

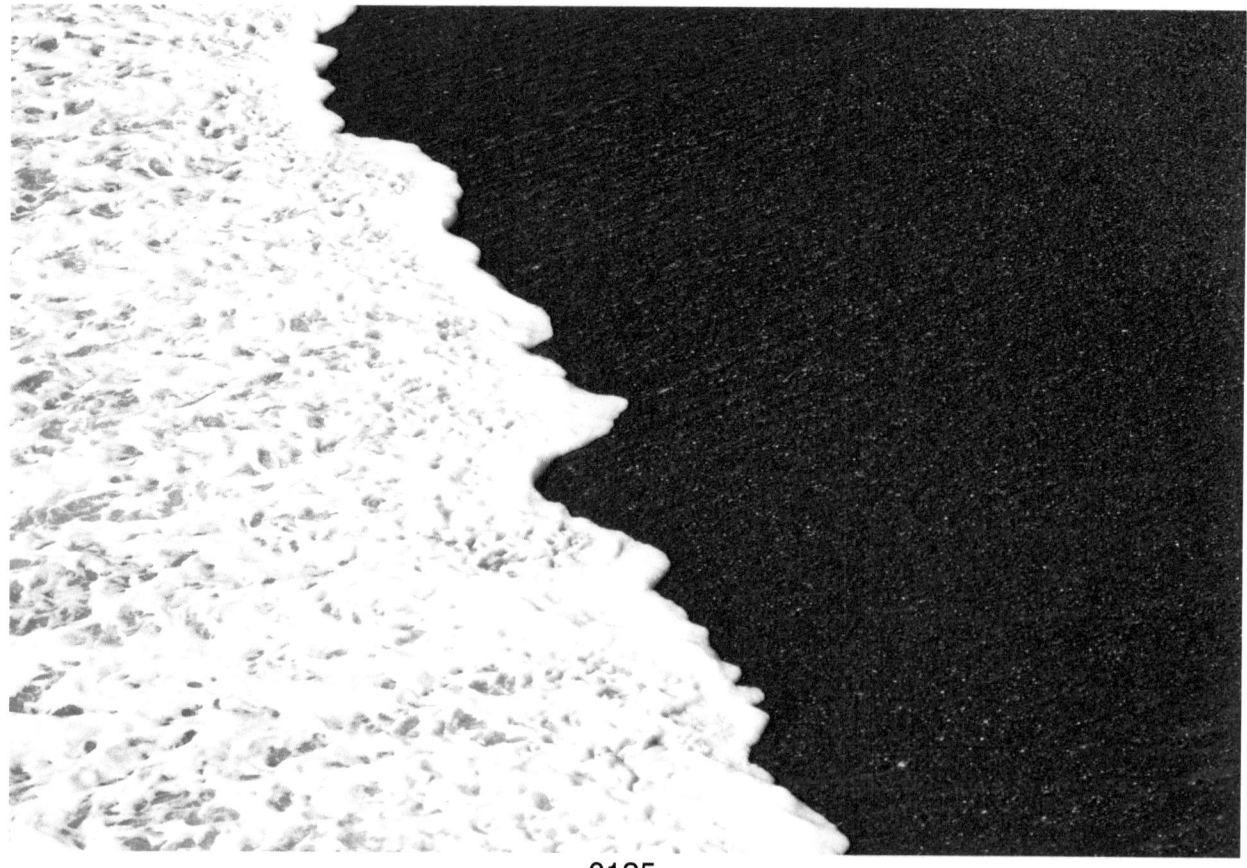

0125

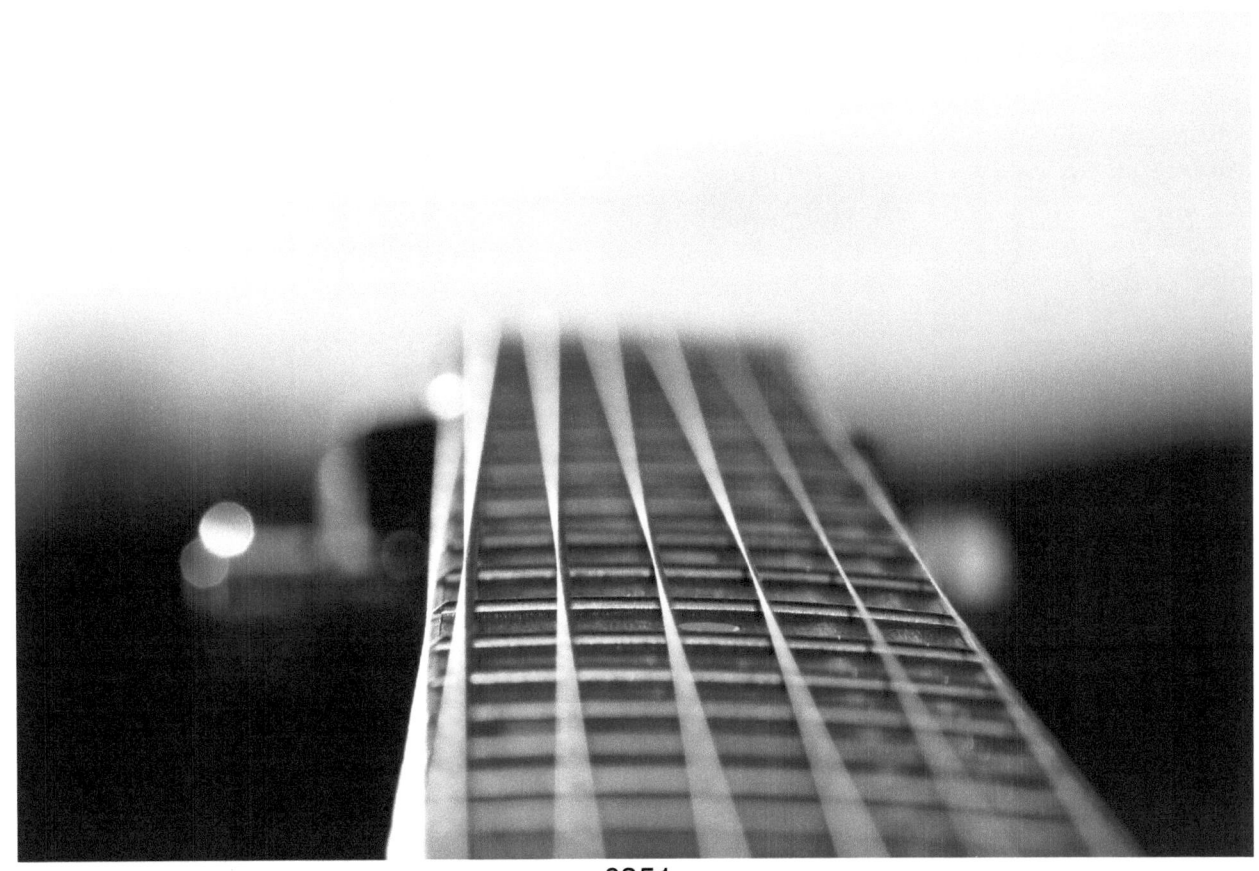

0351

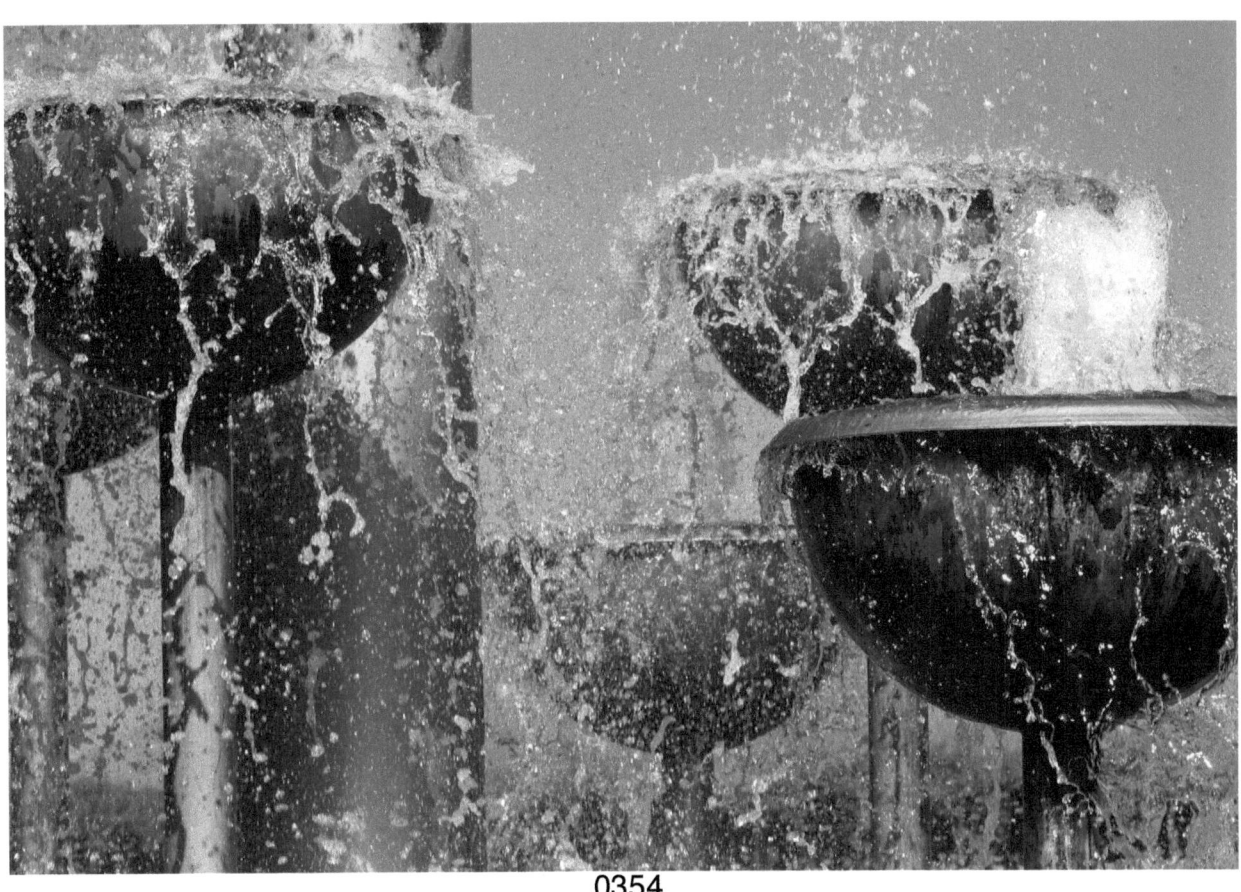

0354

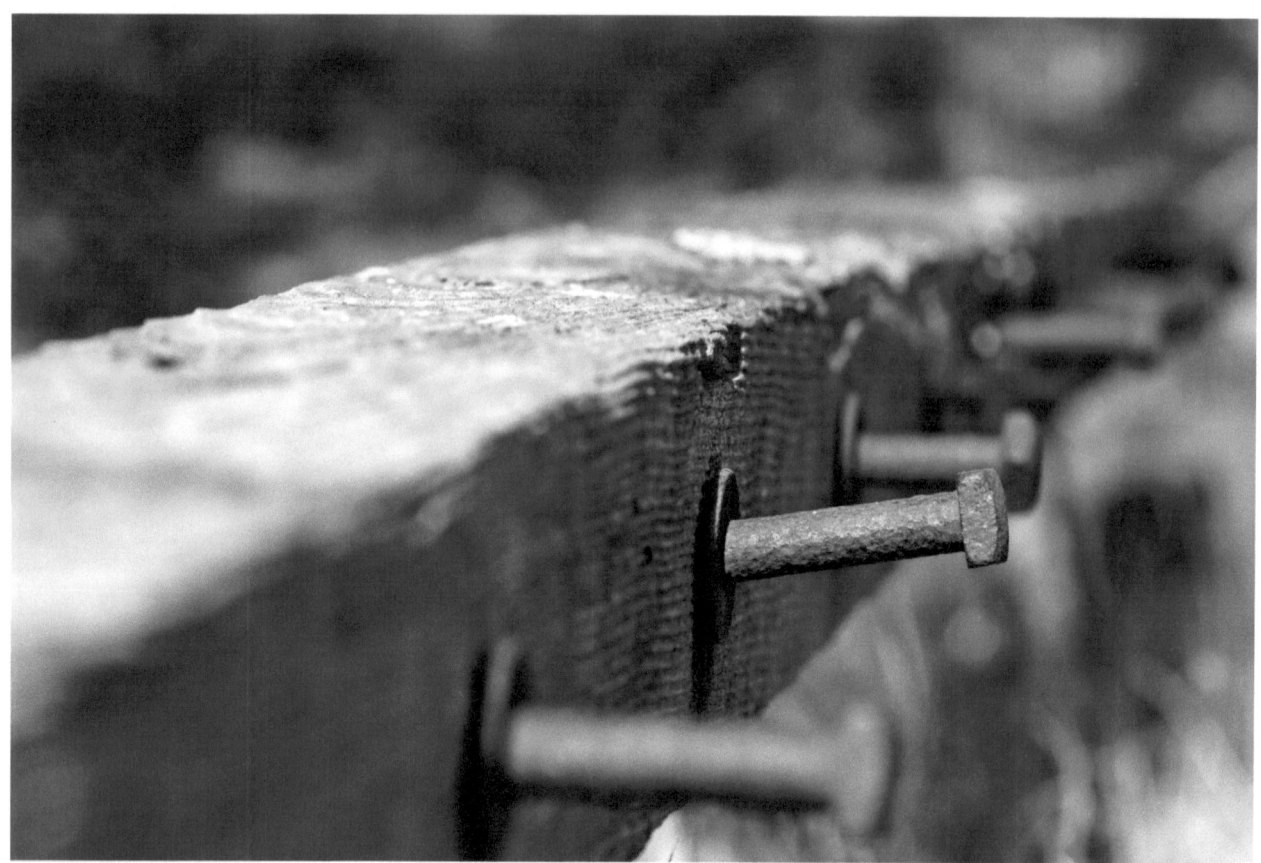

0430

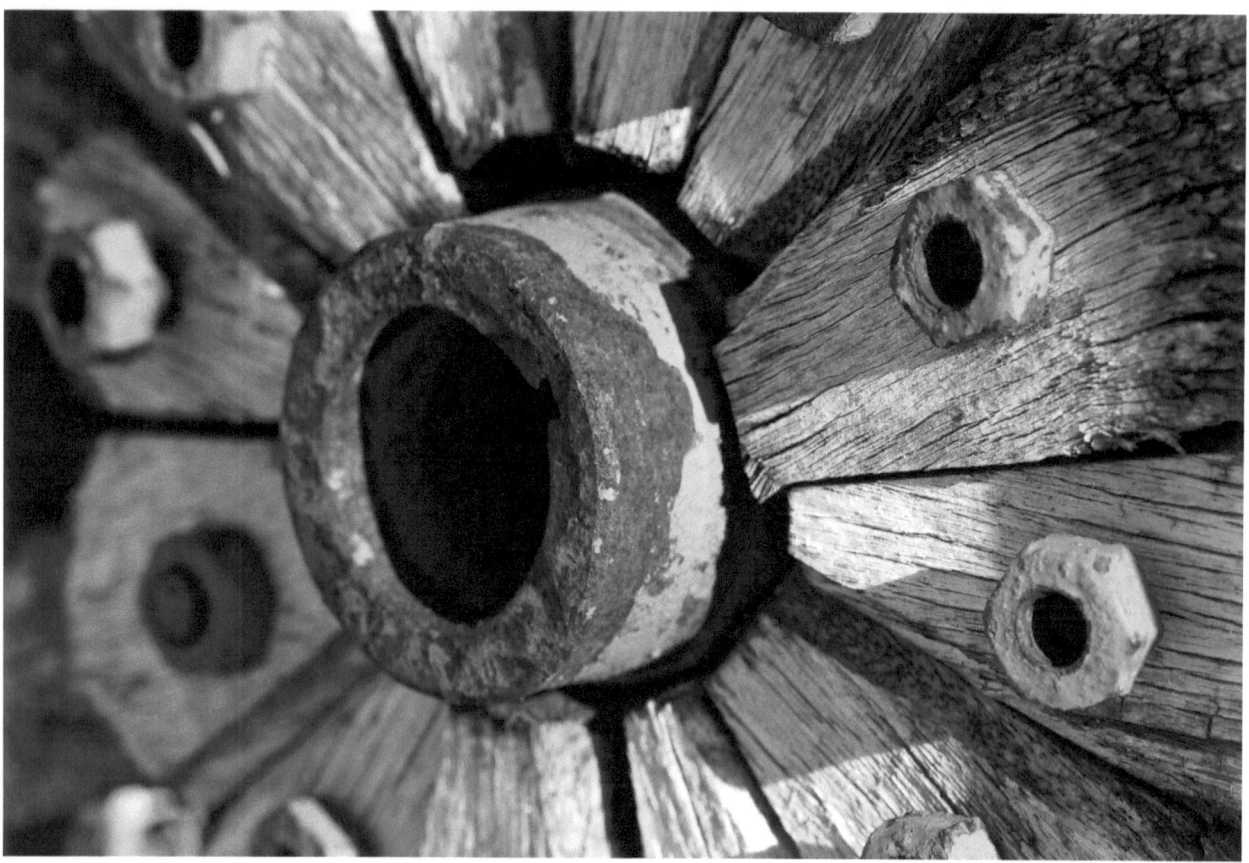

0437

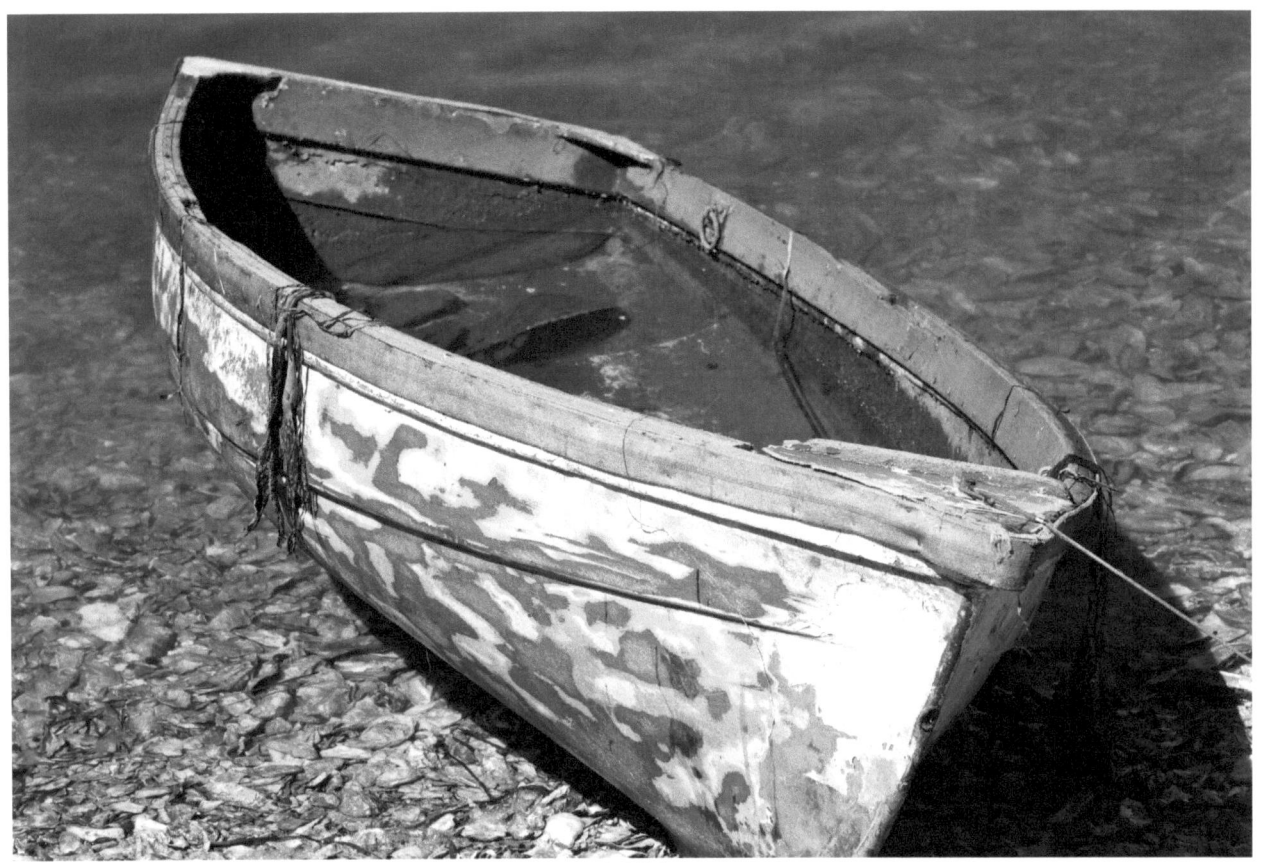

0471

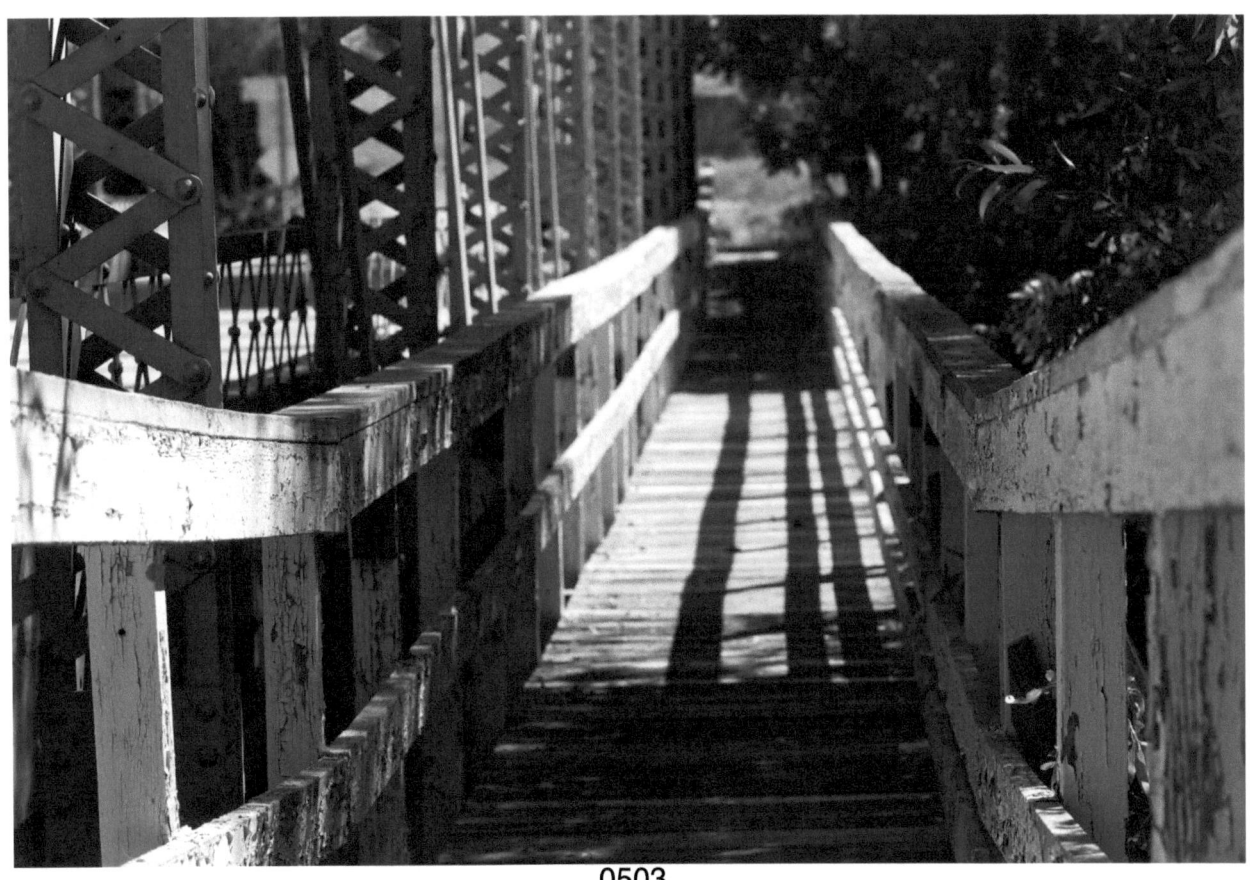

0503

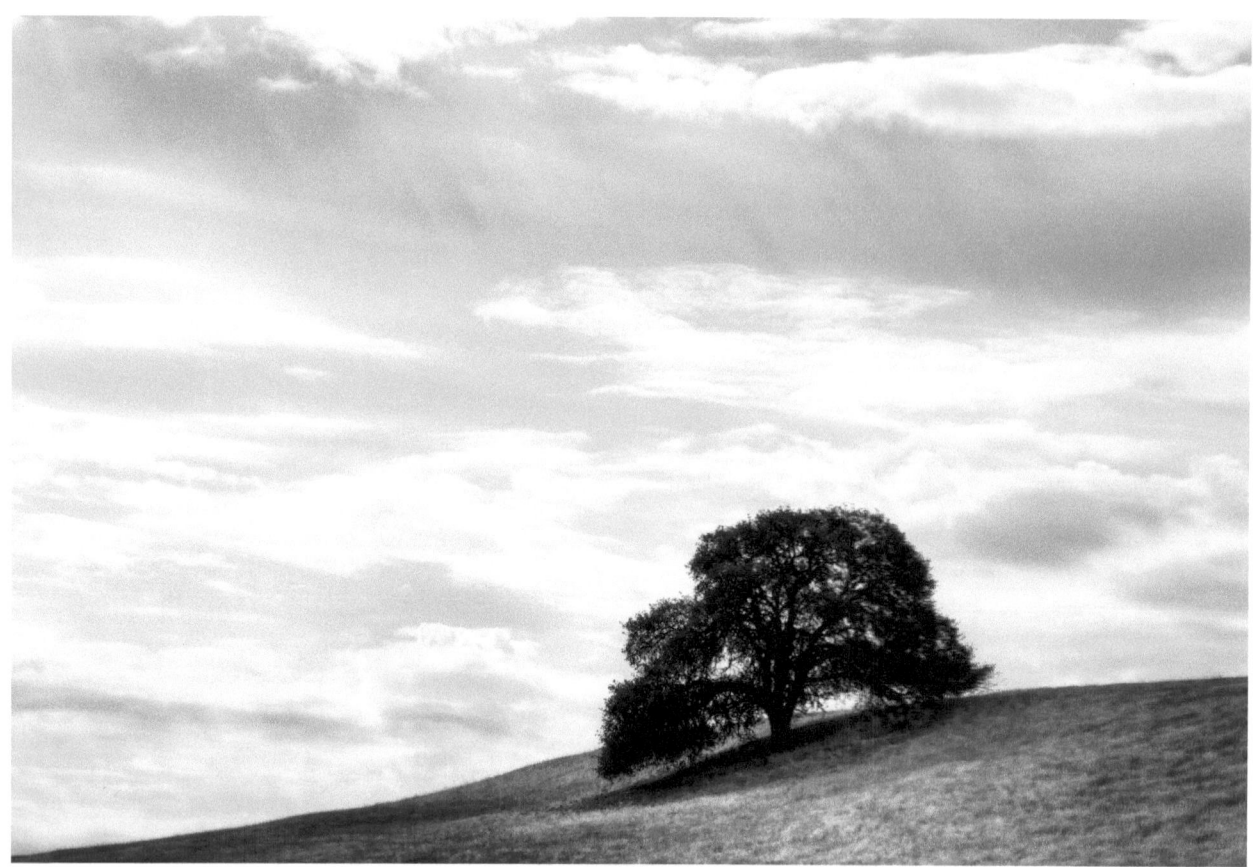

0531

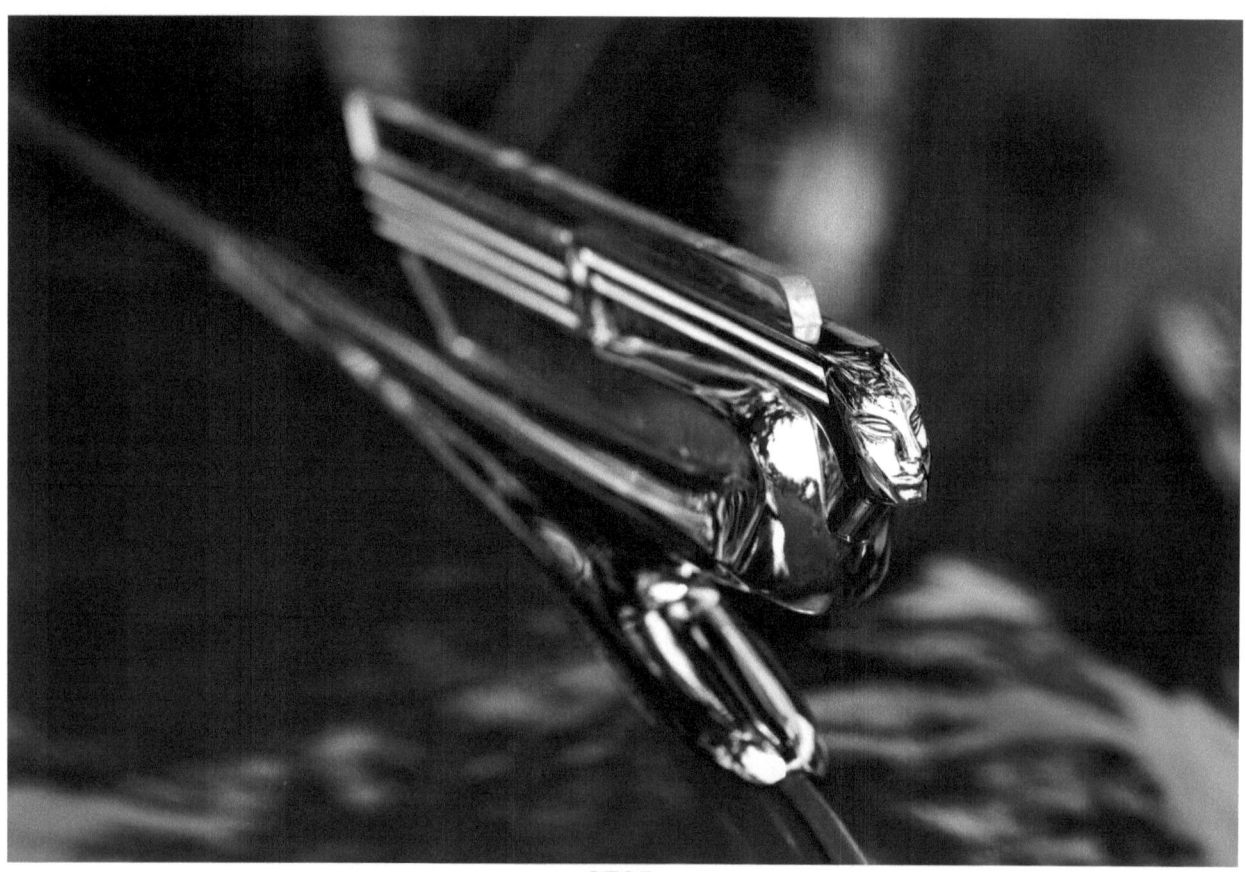

0705

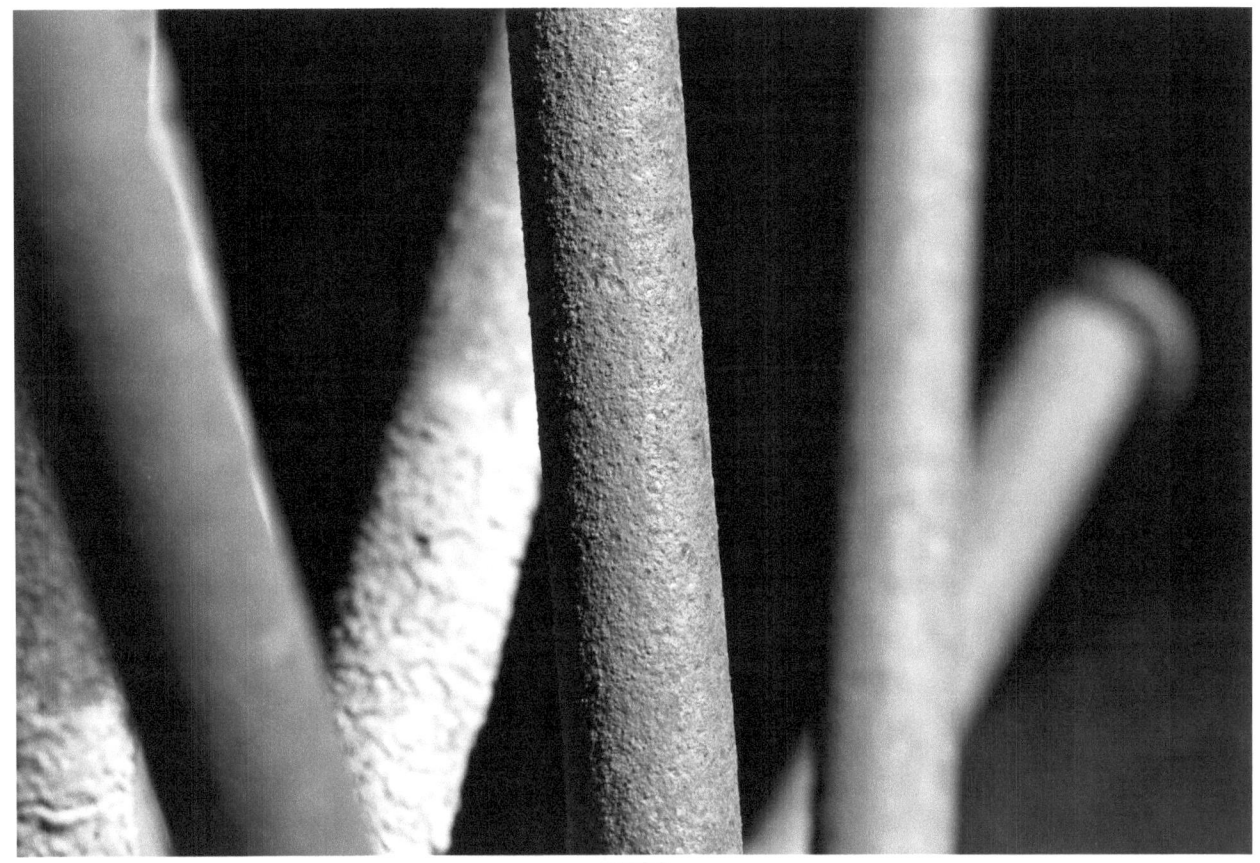

0780

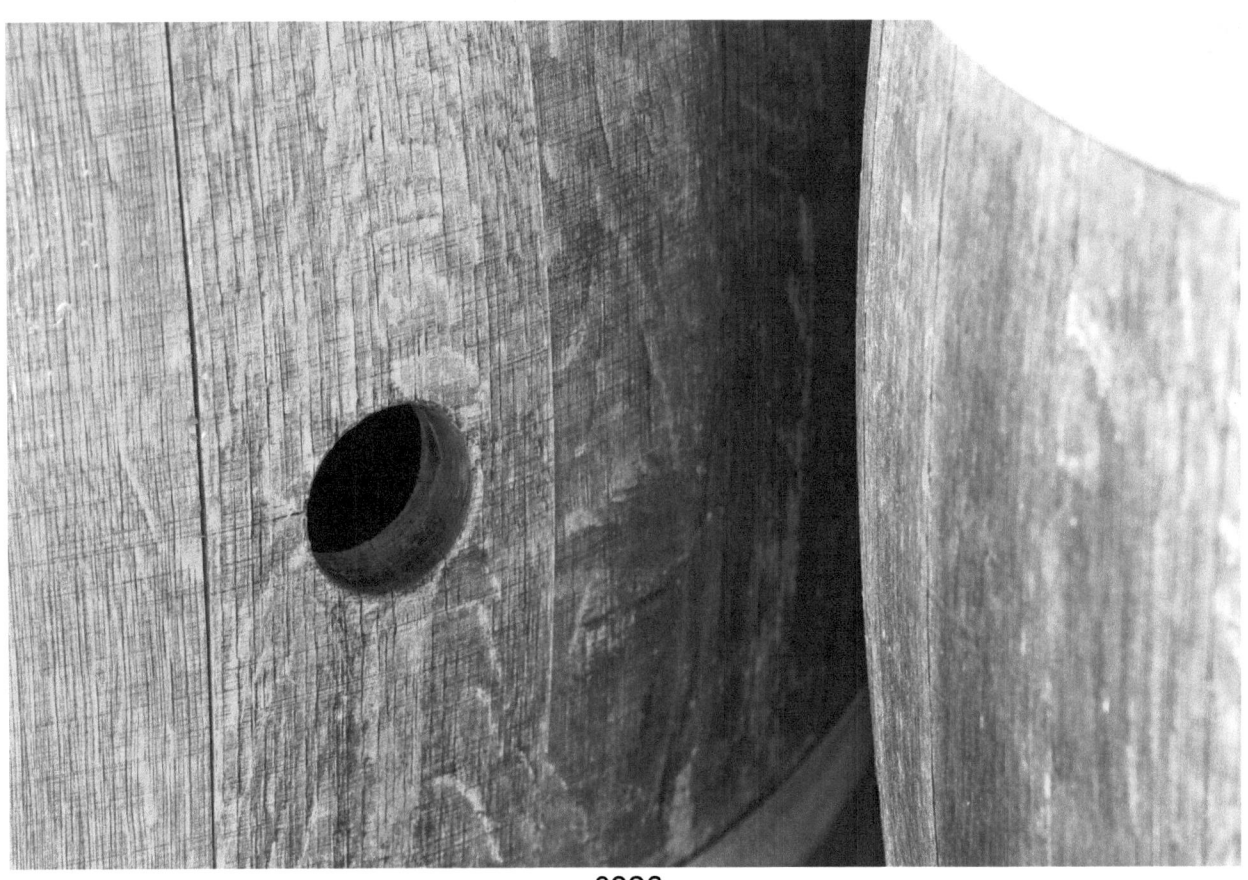

0826

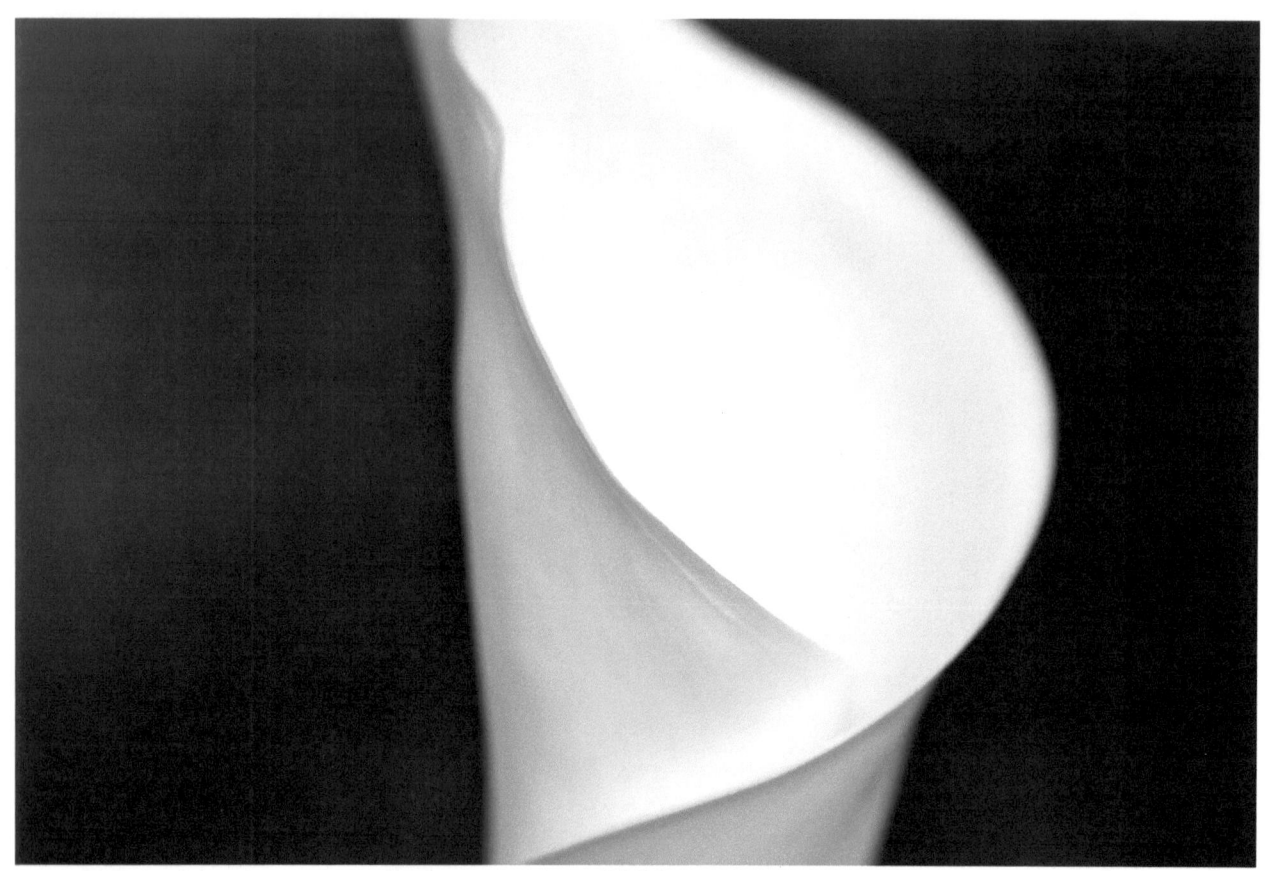

0920

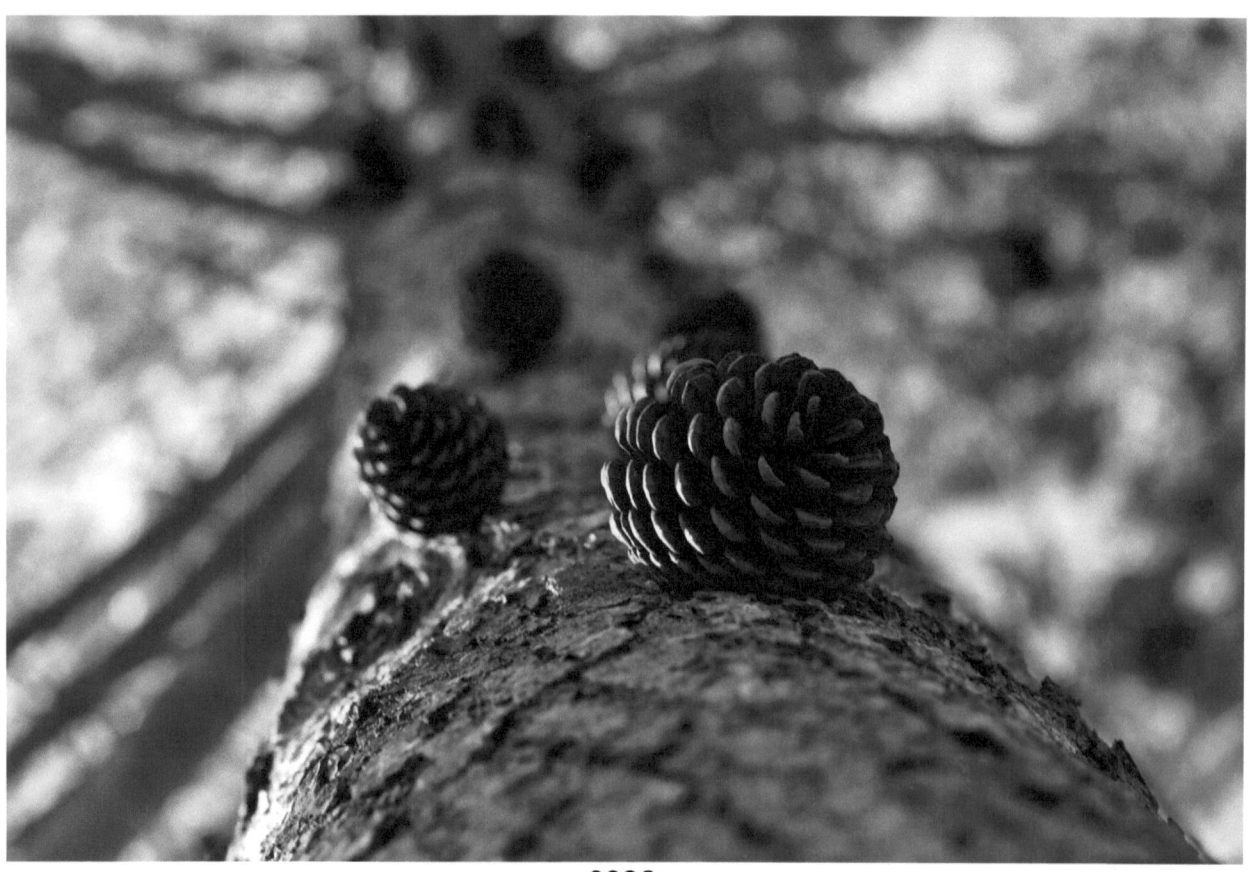

0938

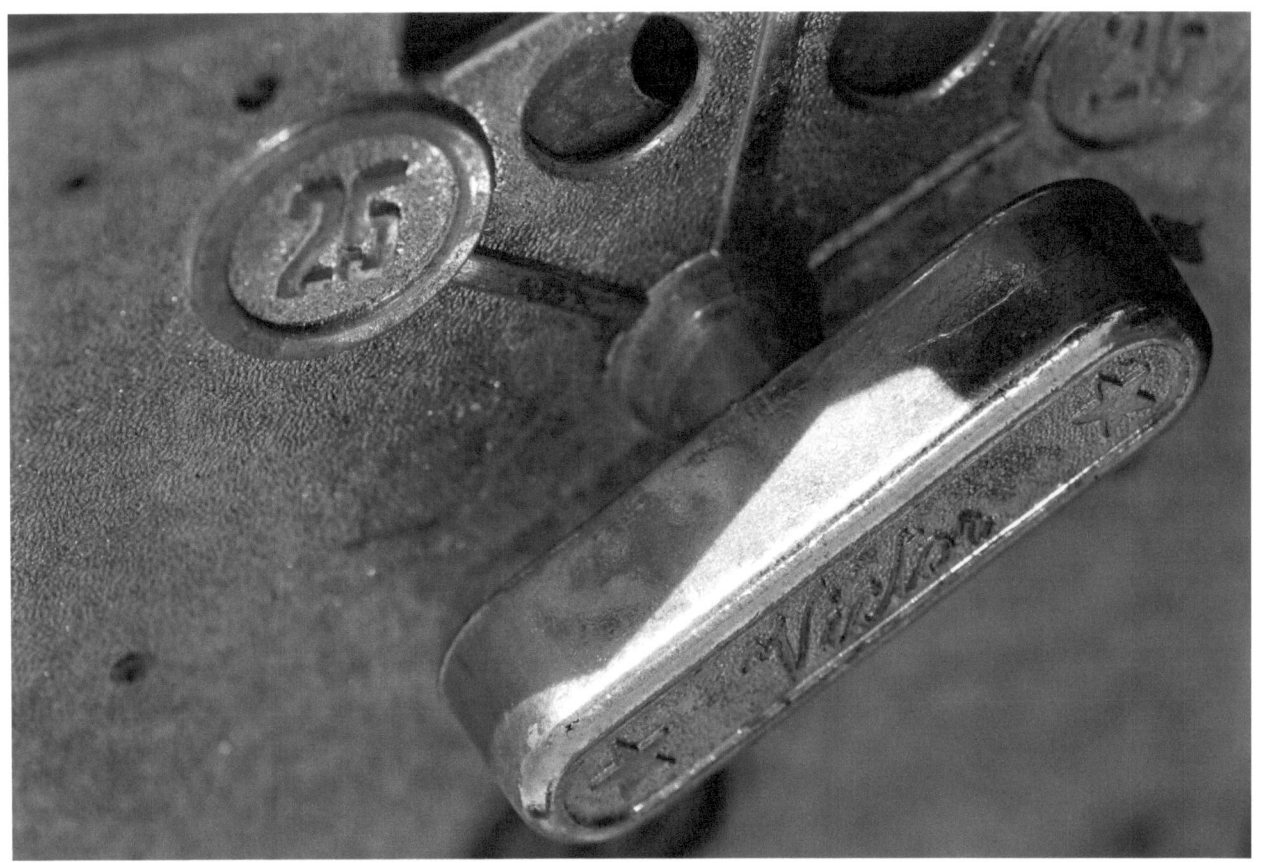

1085

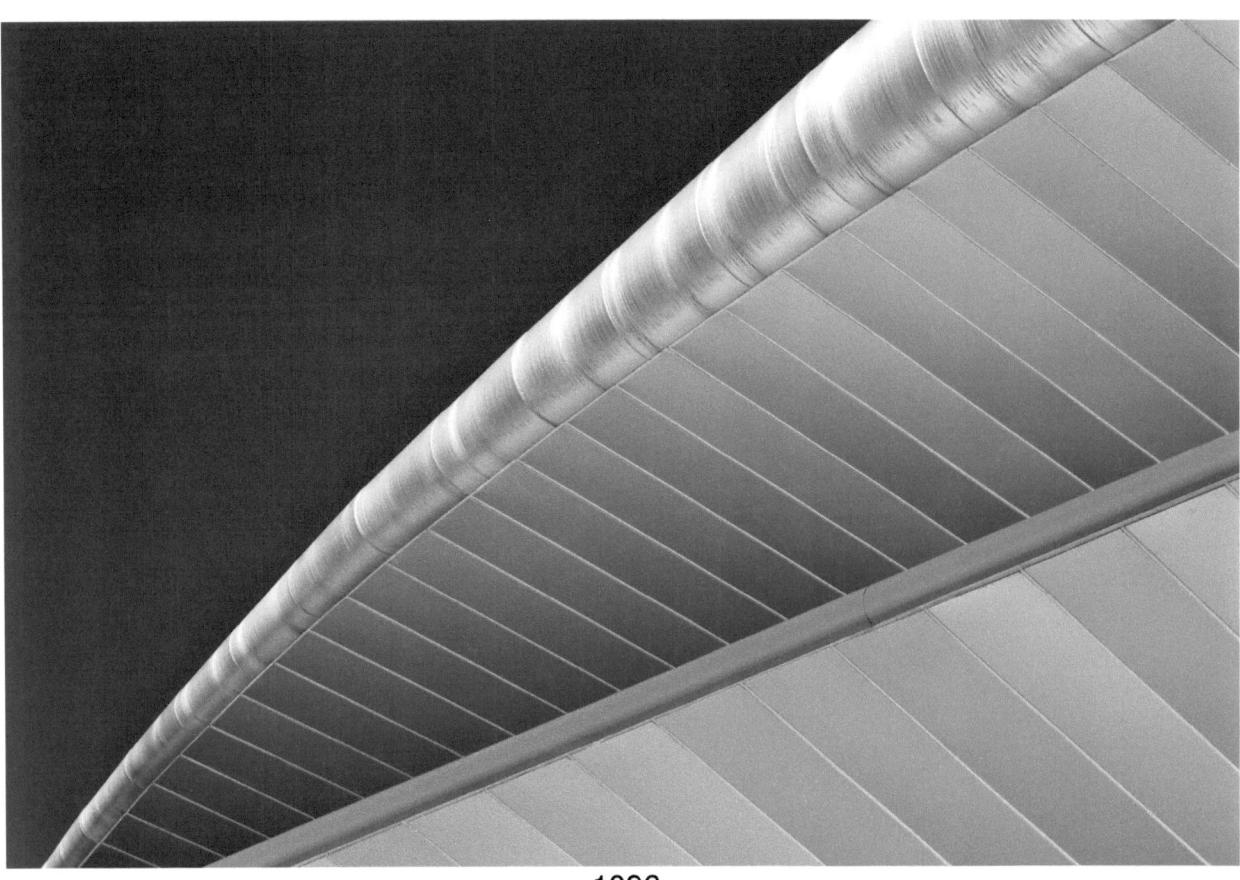

1096

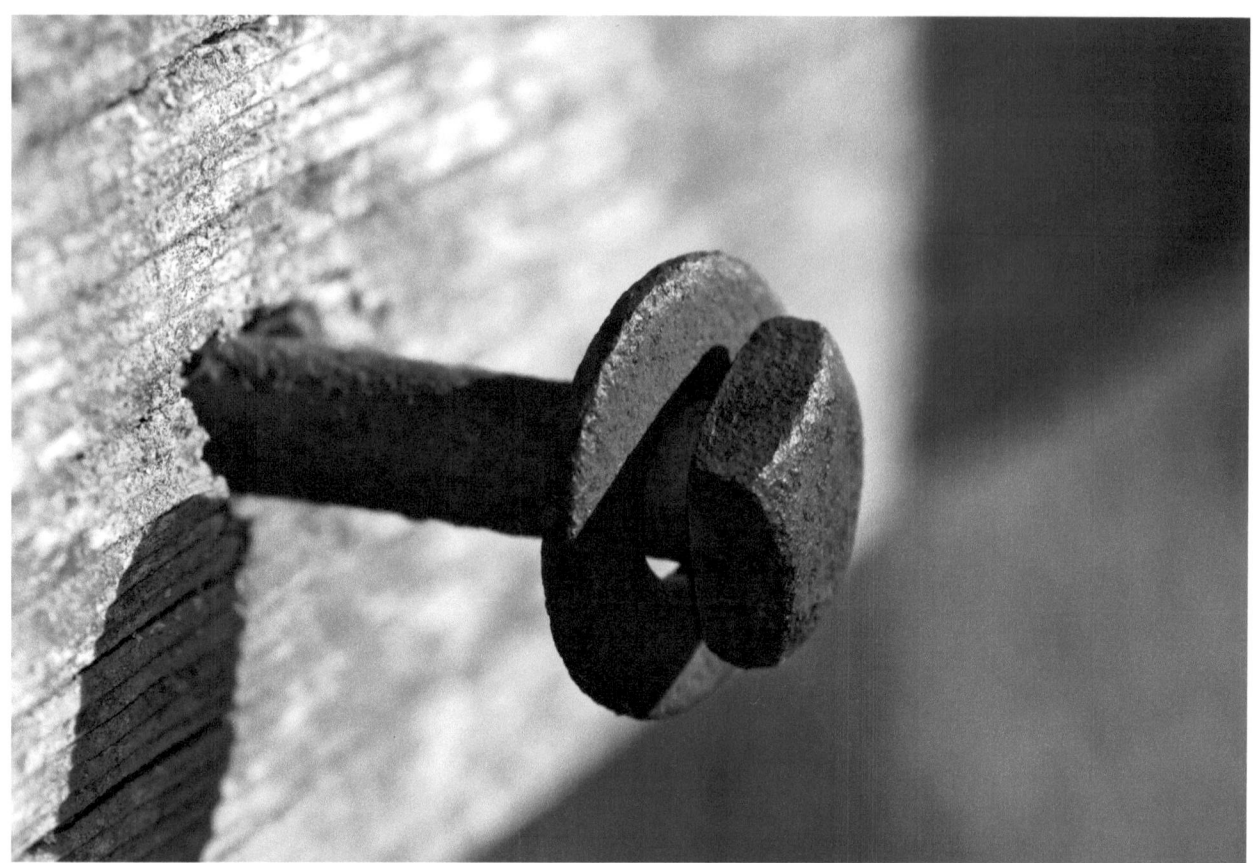

1173

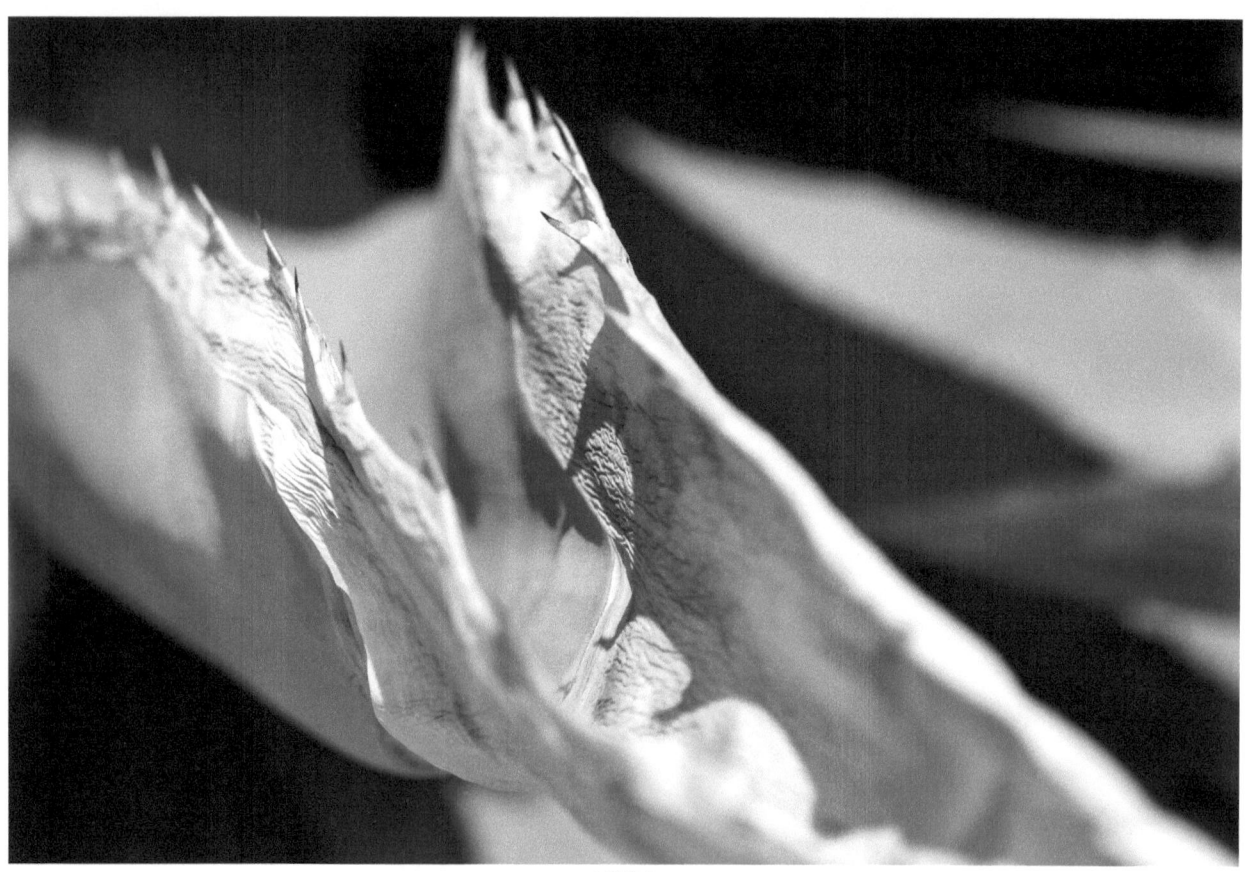

1581

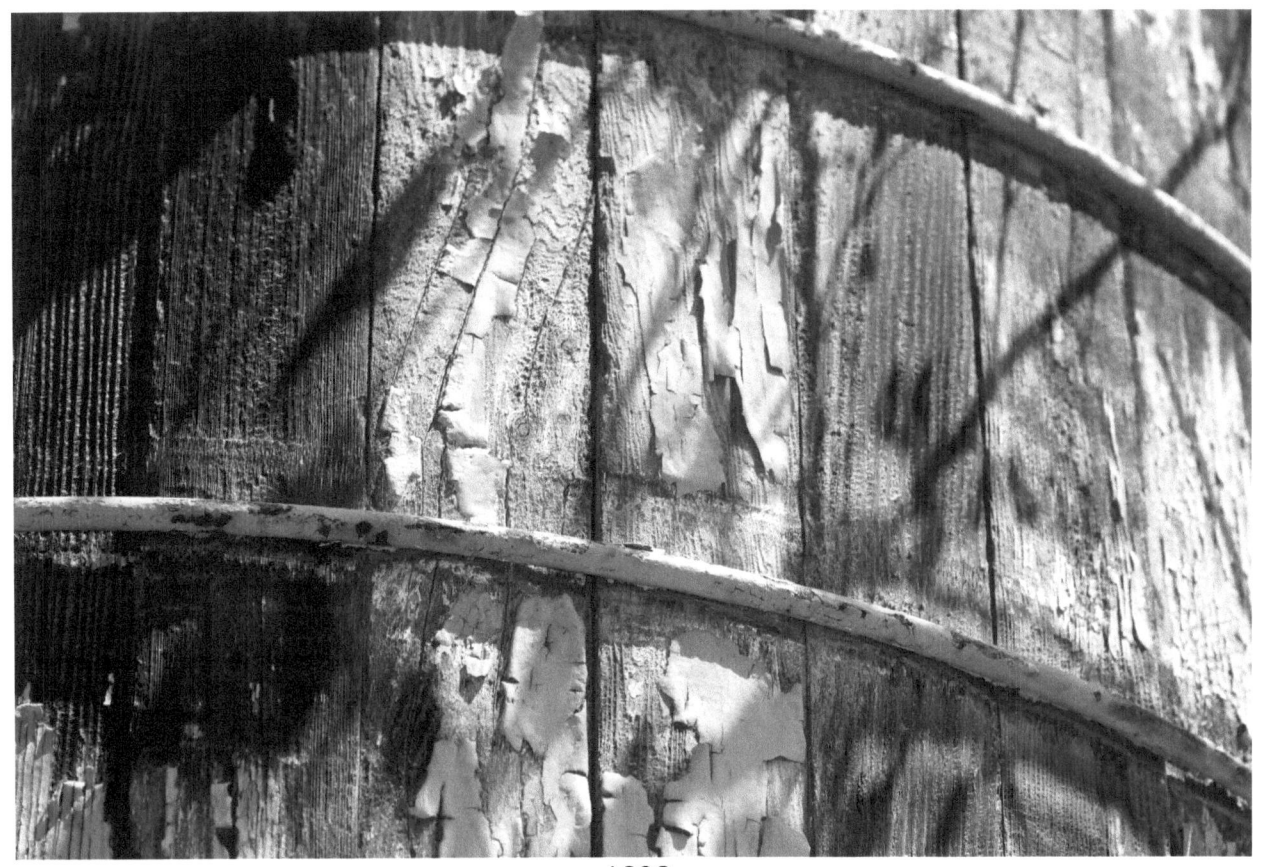
1608

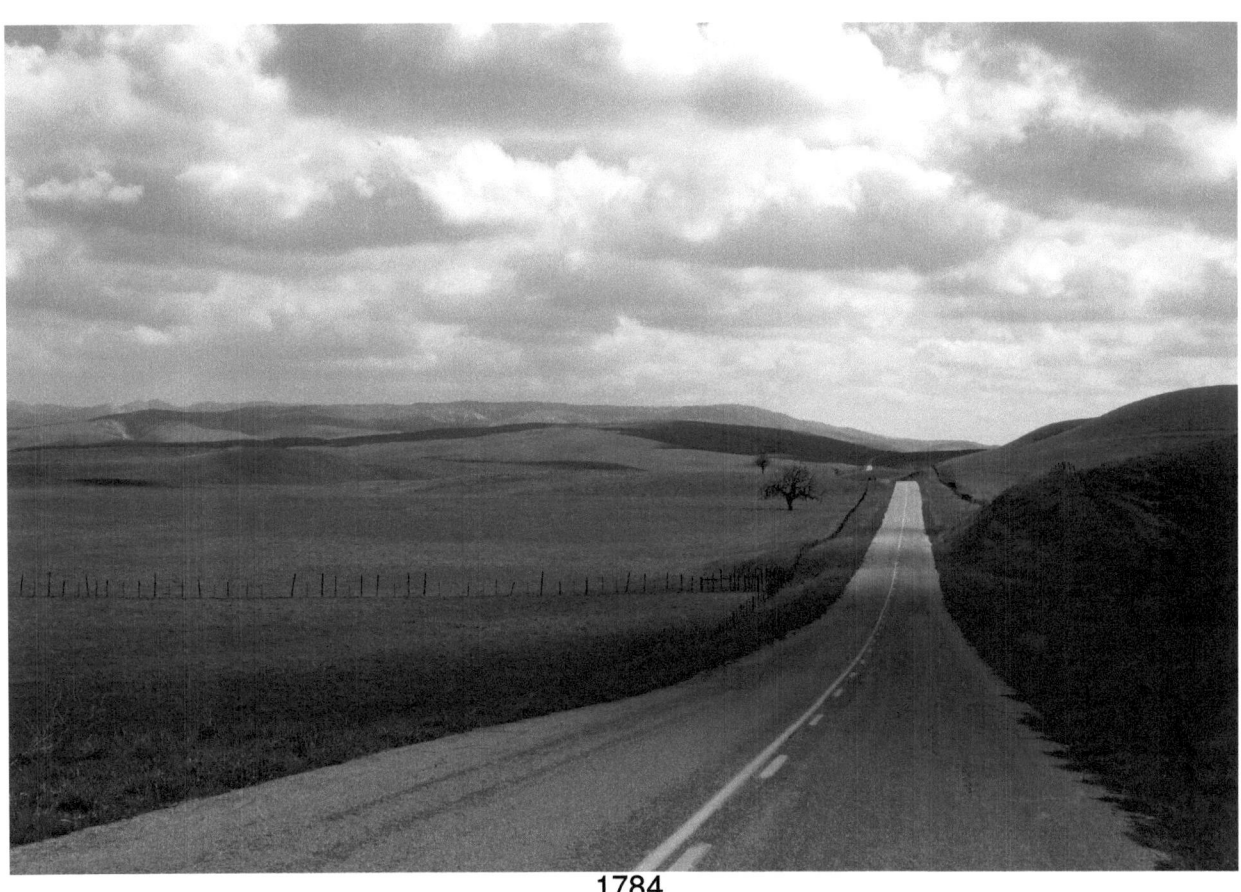
1784

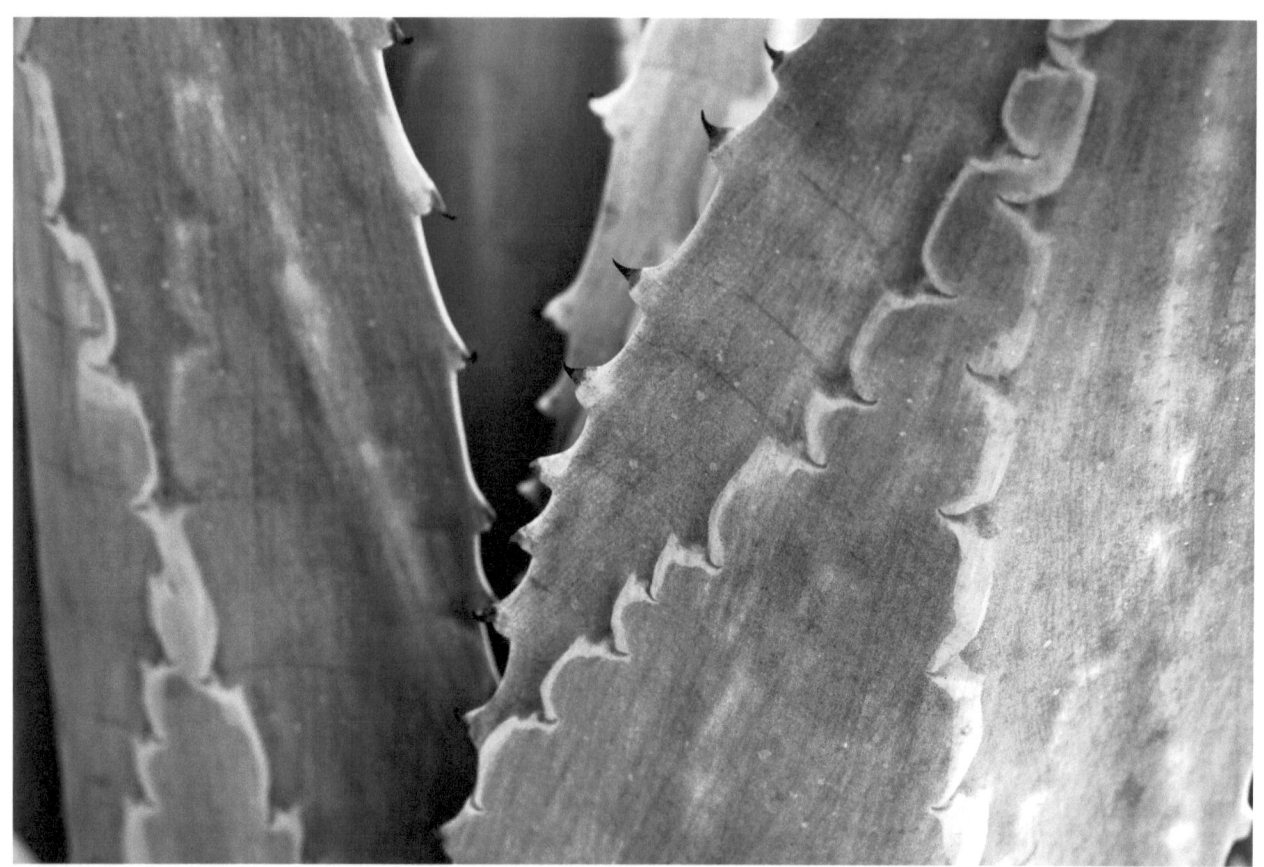

1976

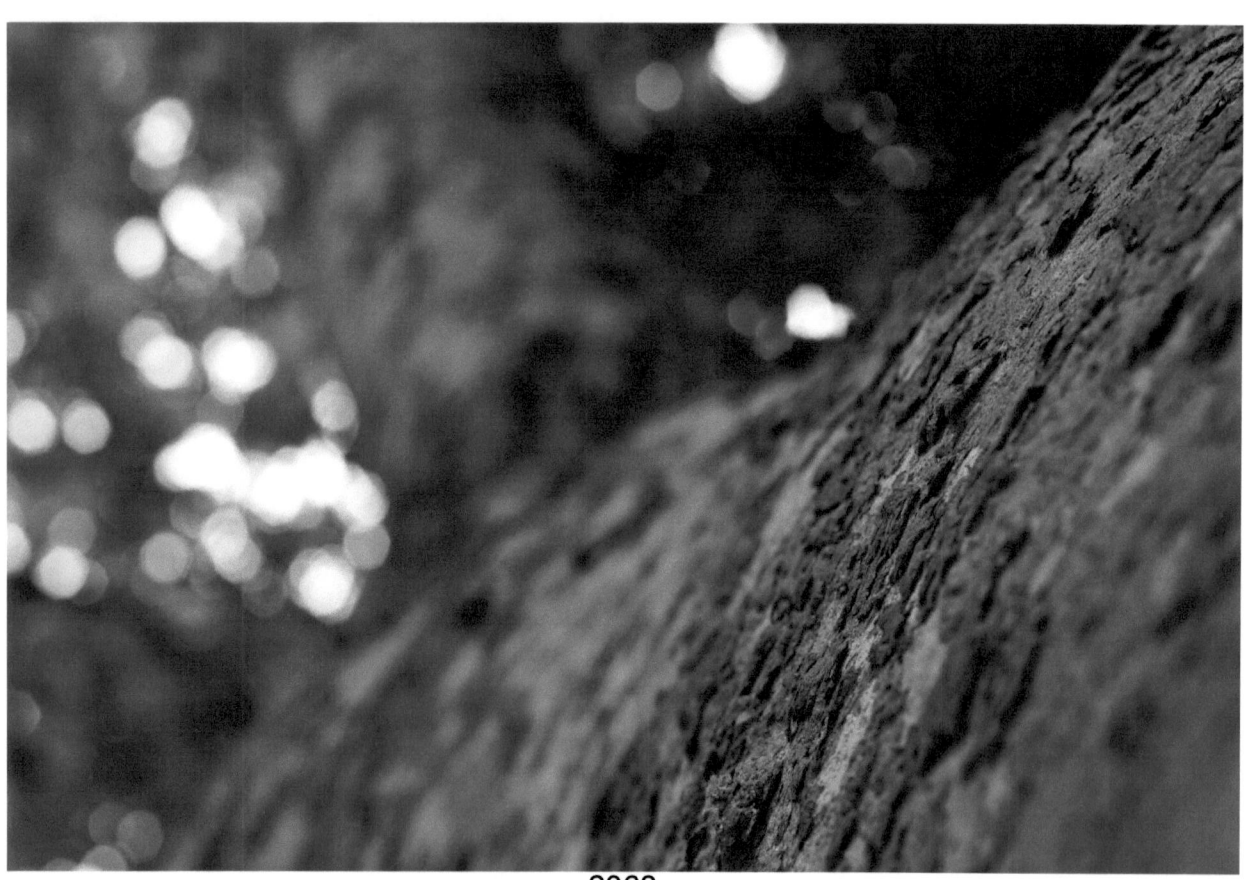

2068

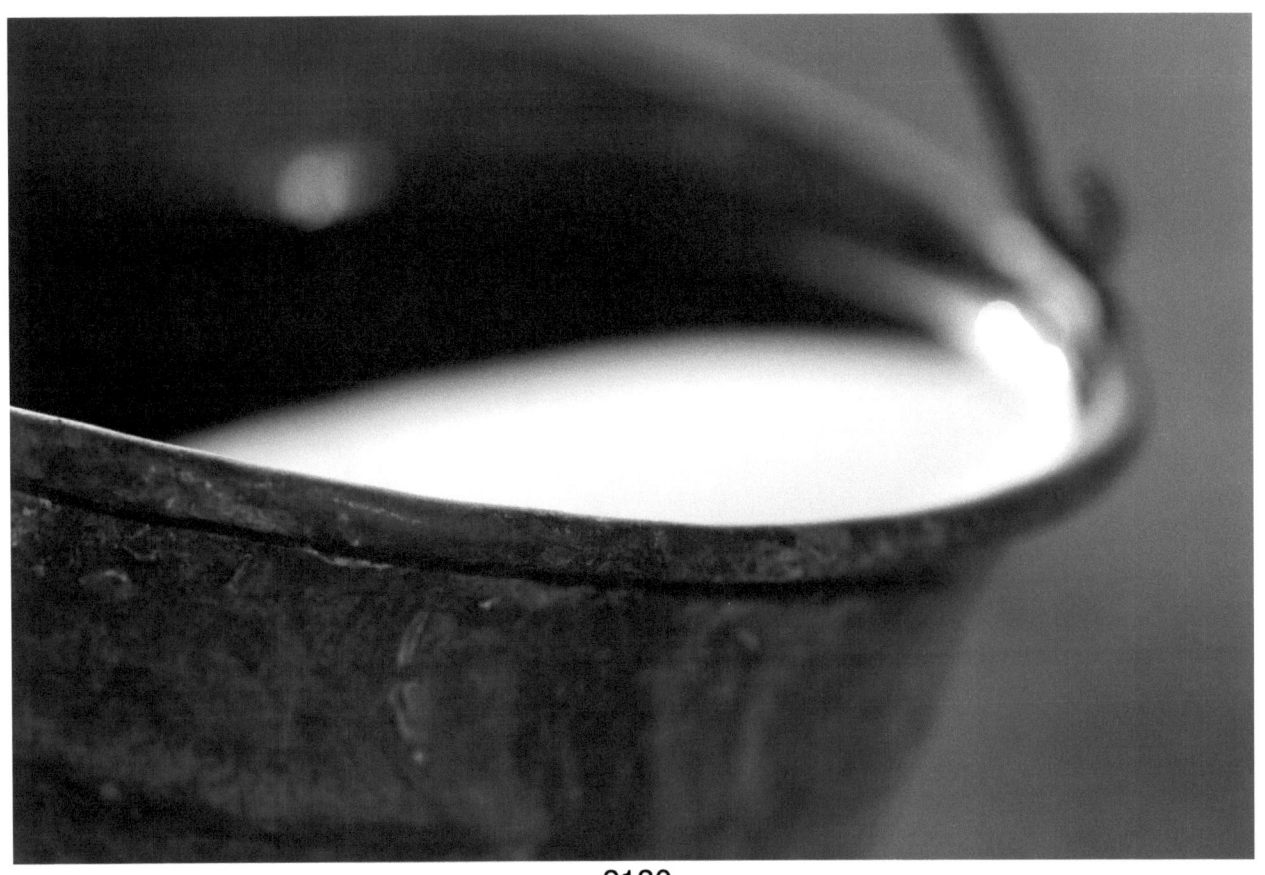

2180

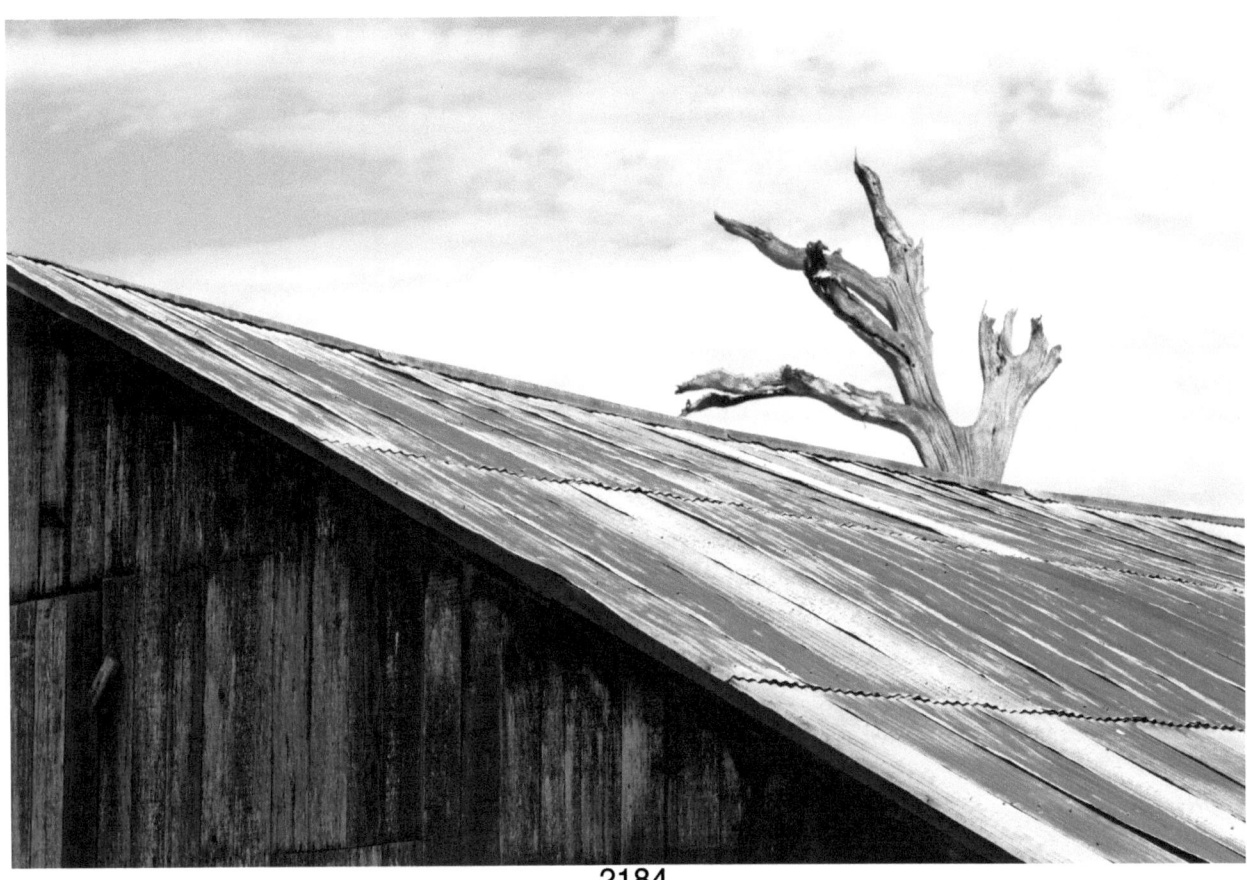

2184

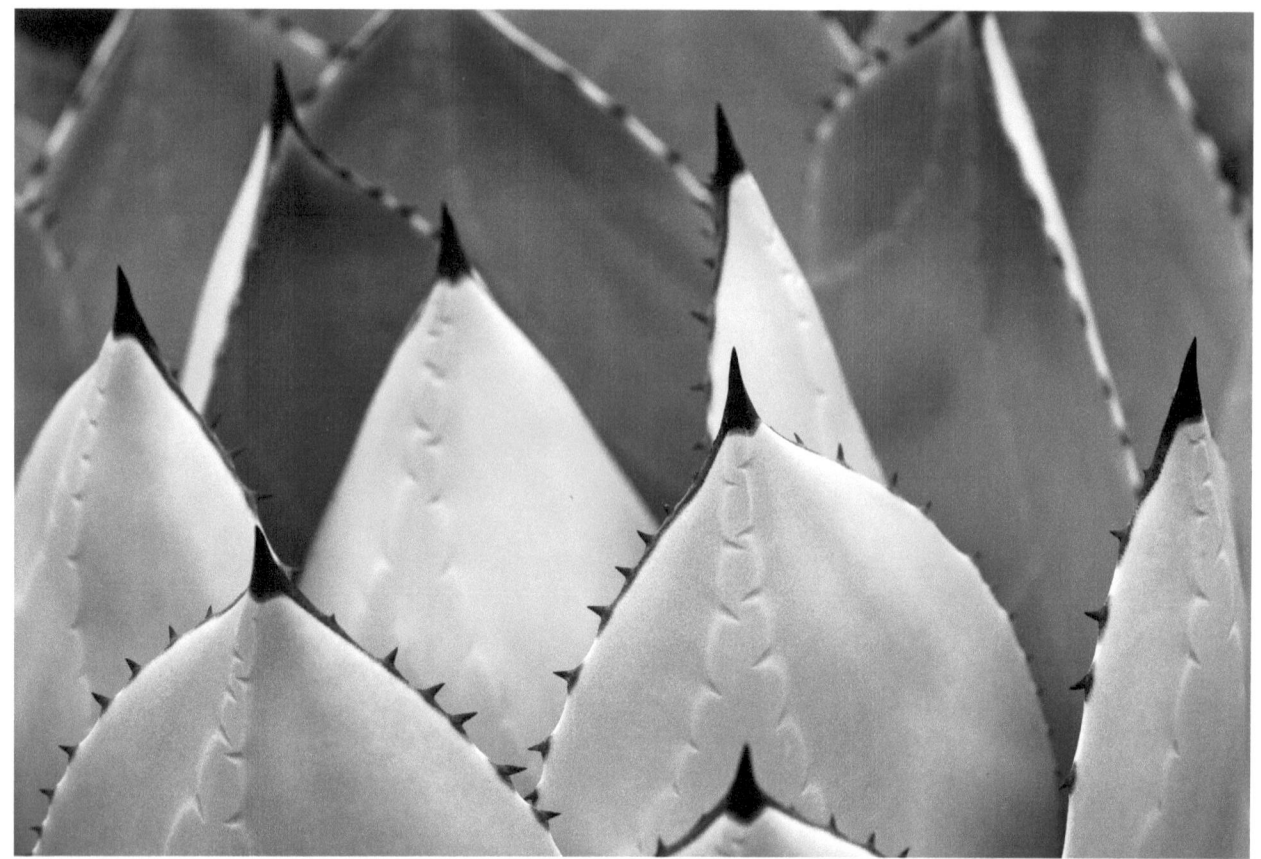

2294

2397

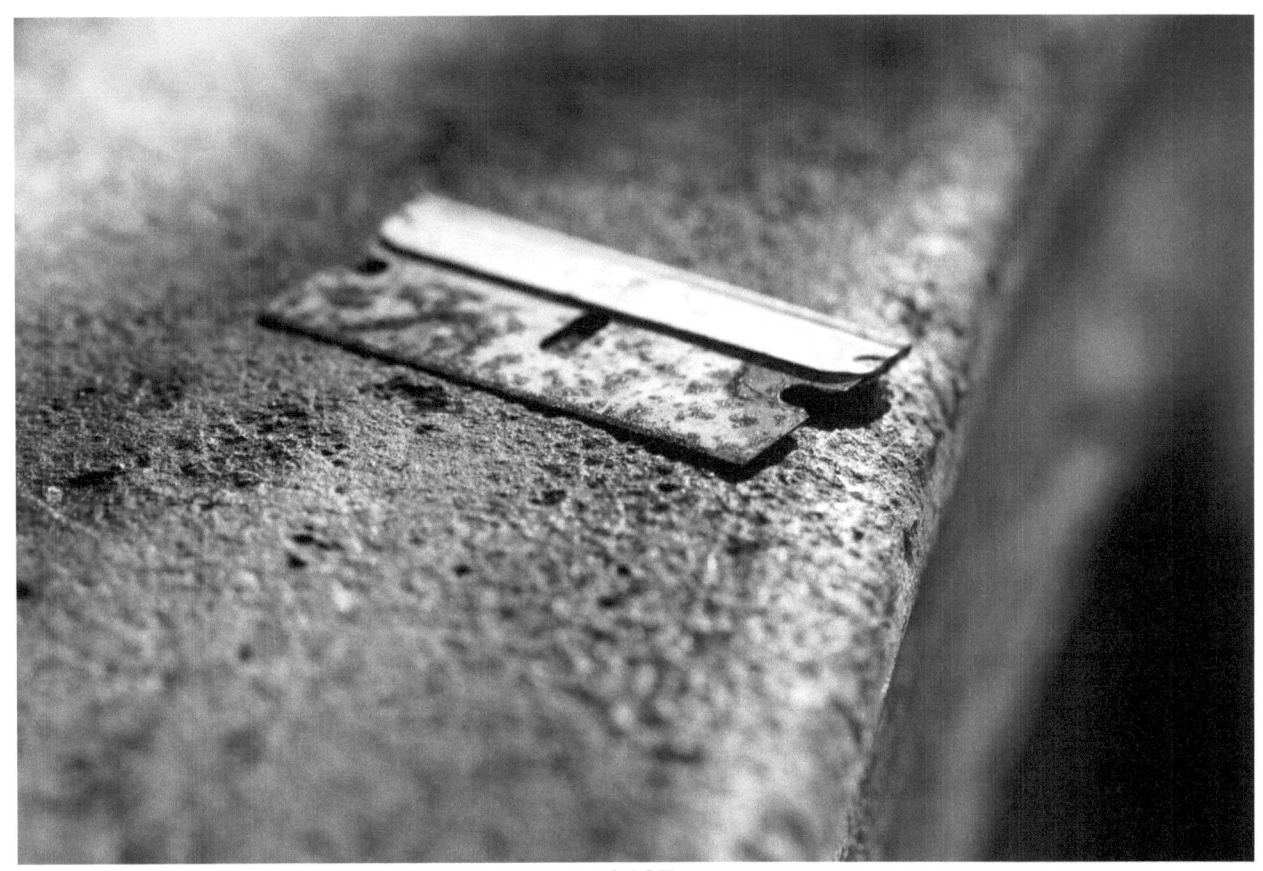

2467

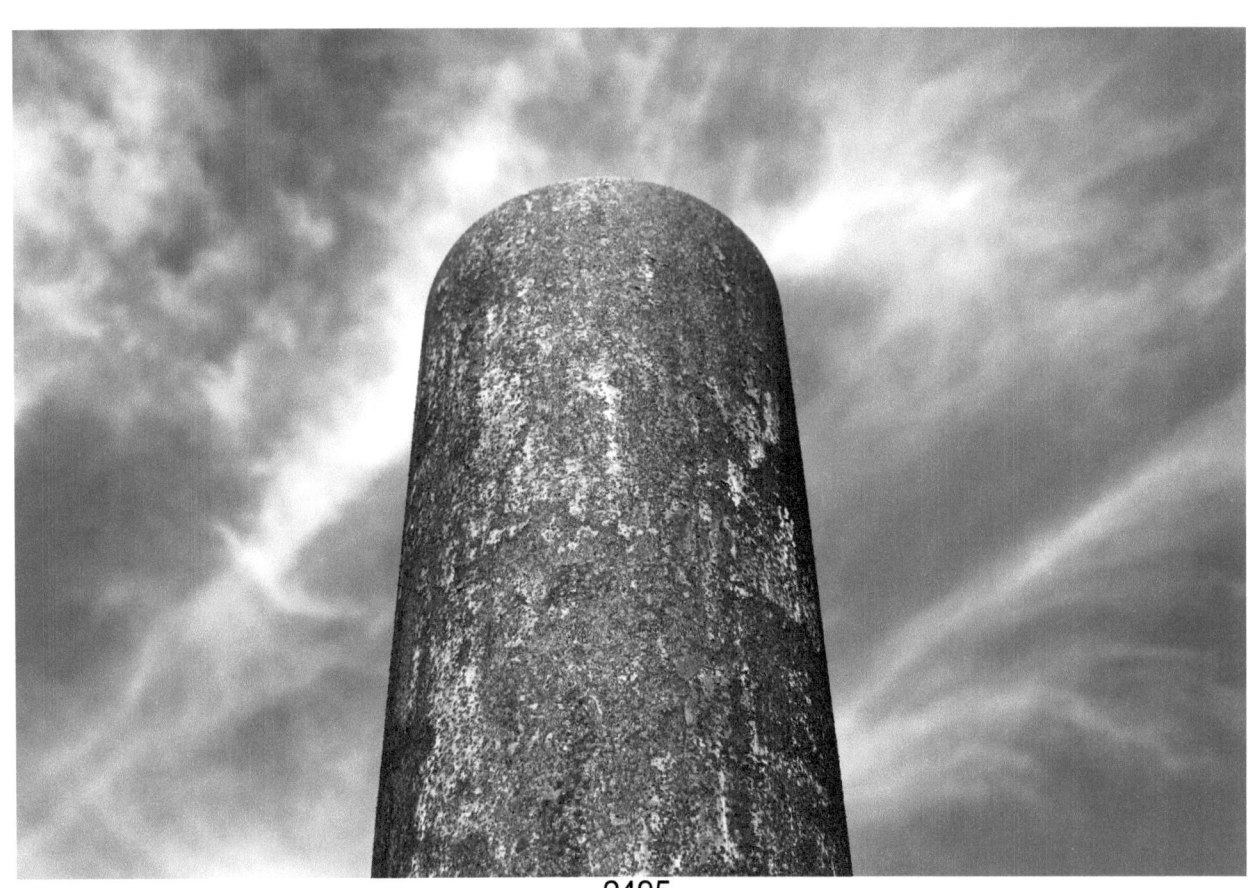

2495

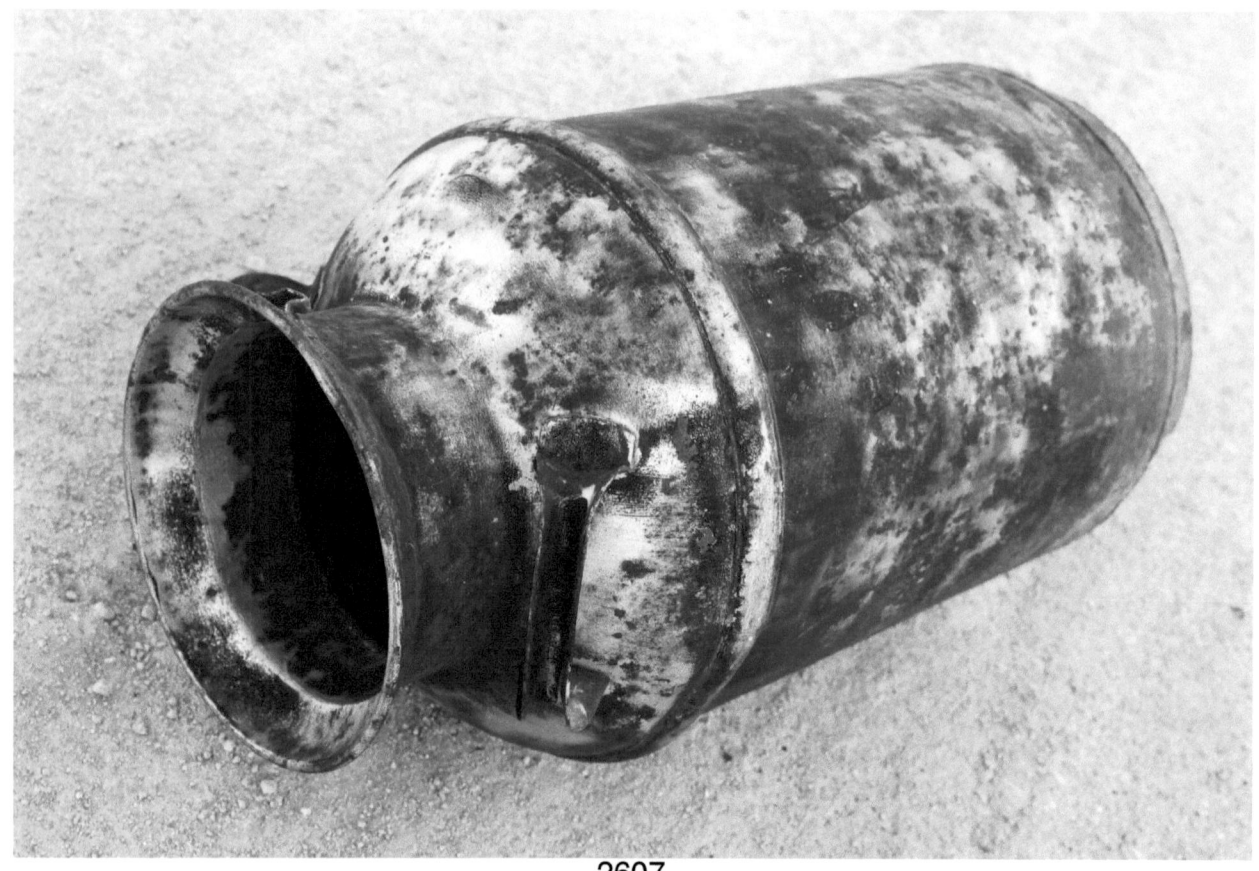

2607

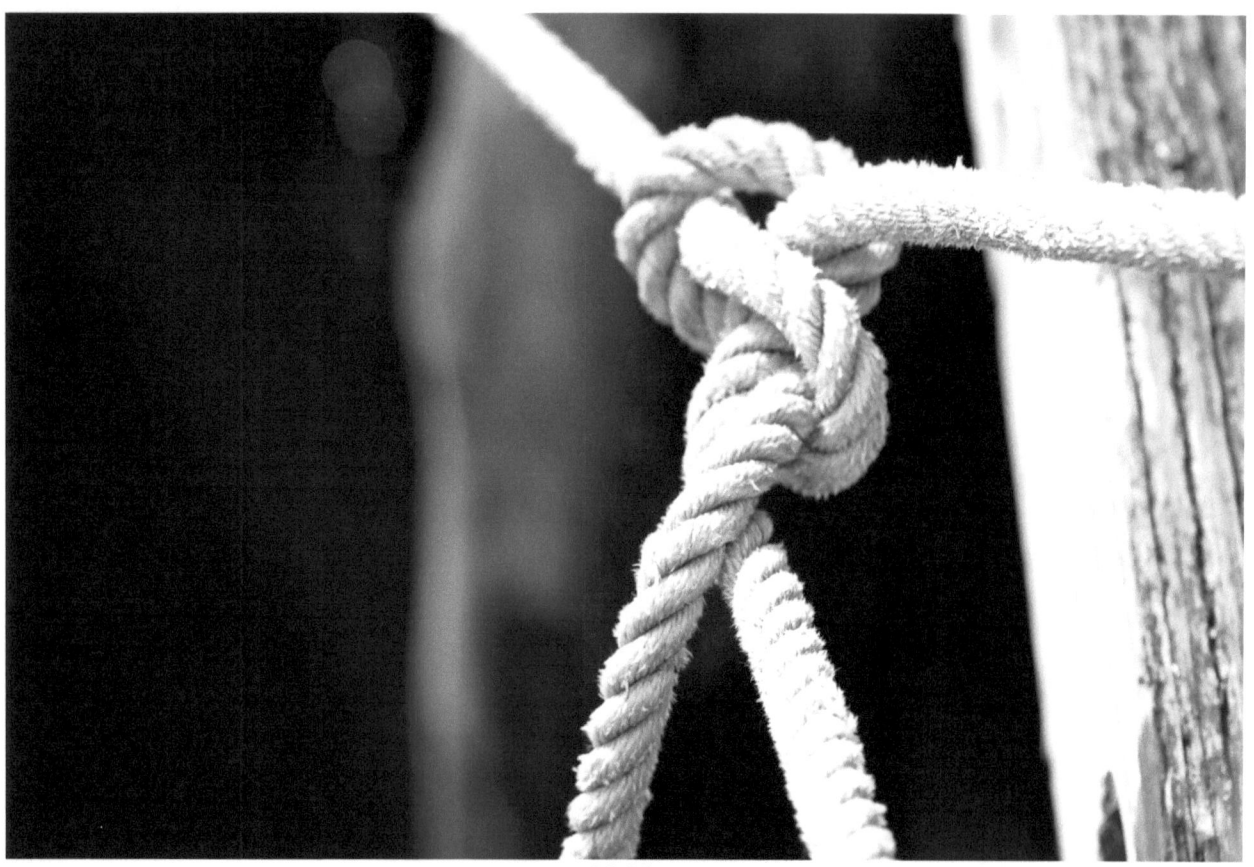

2686

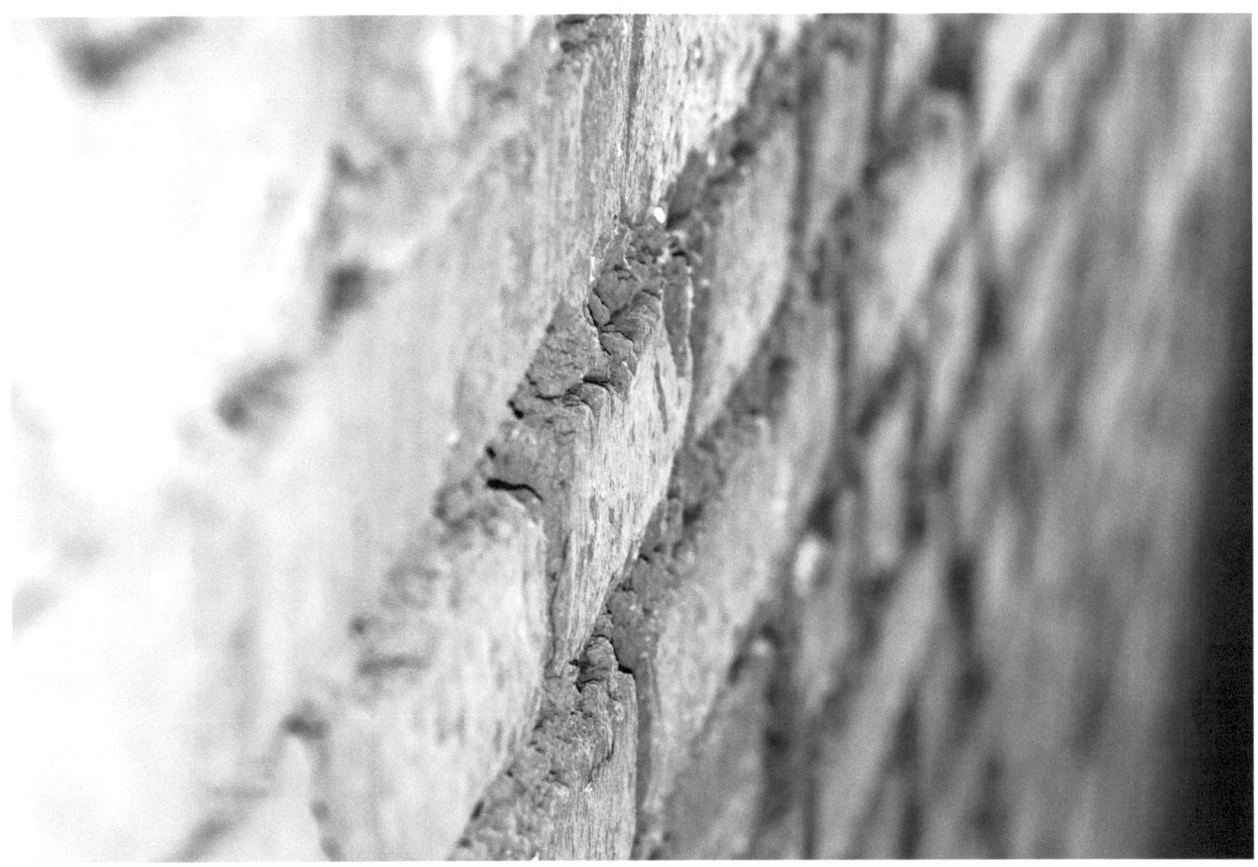

2688

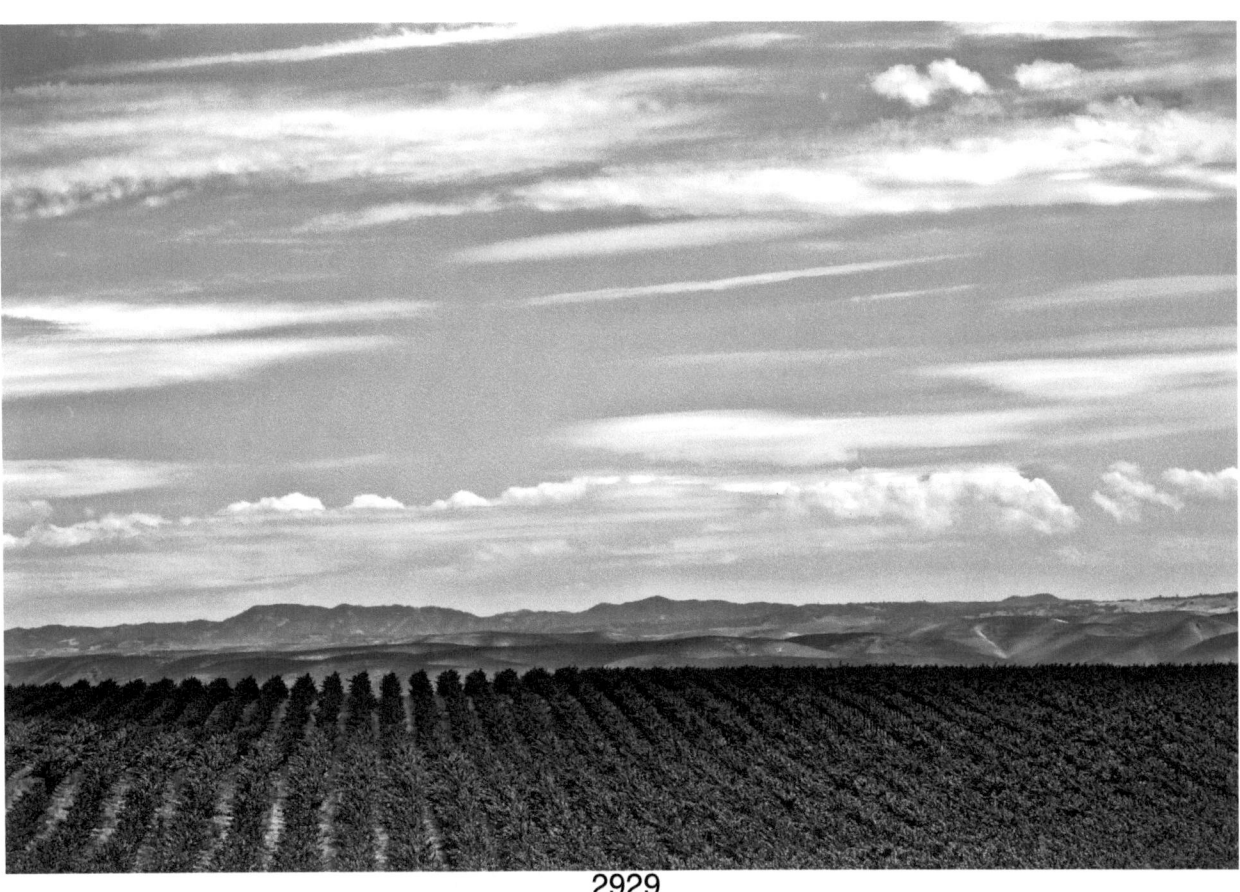

2929

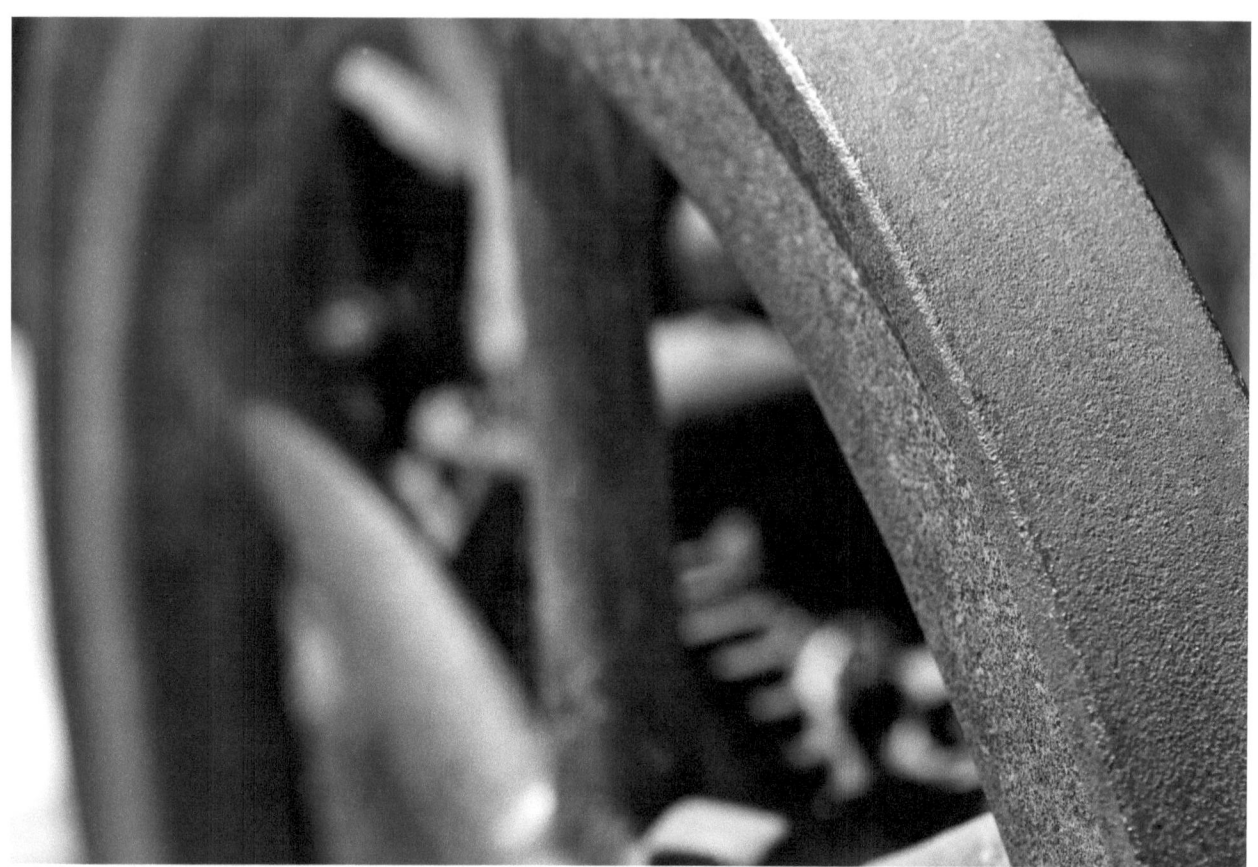

2962

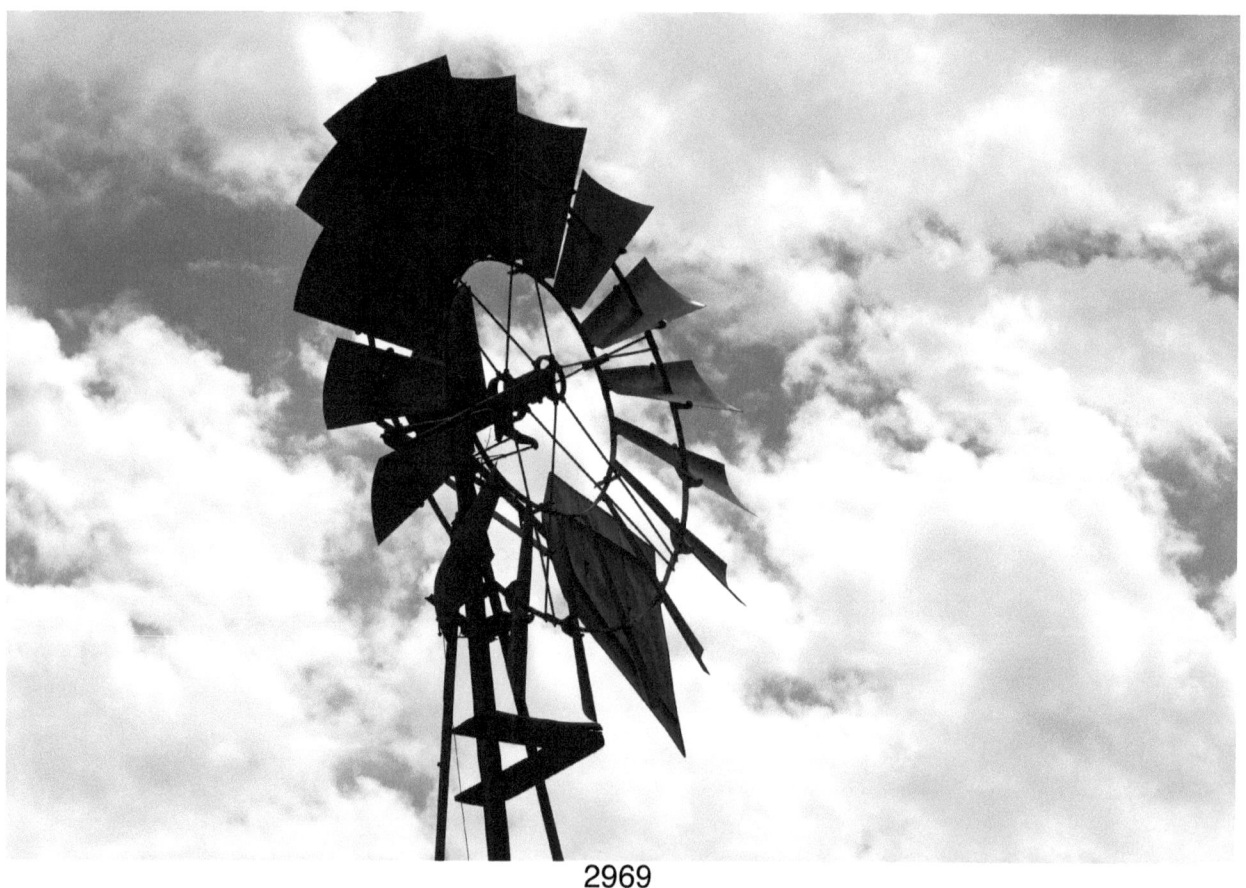

2969

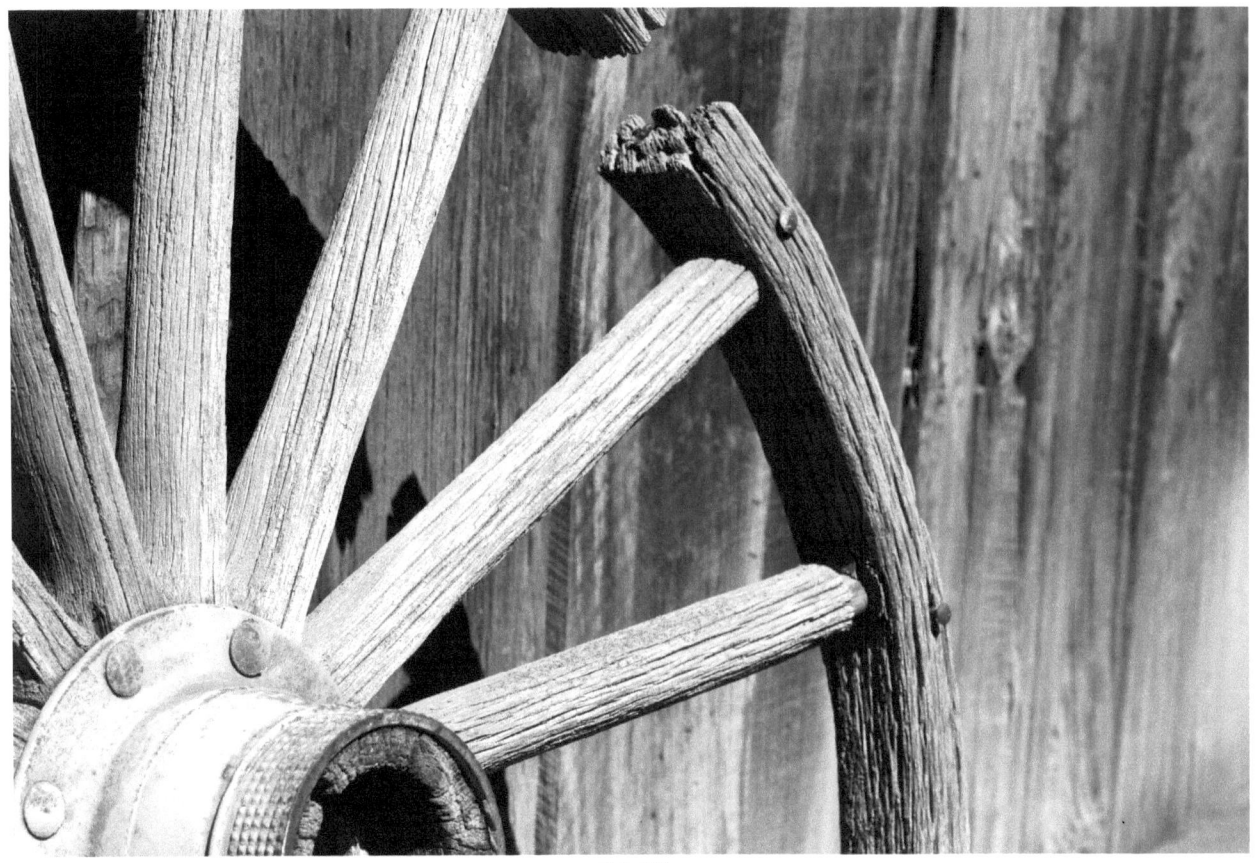

3147

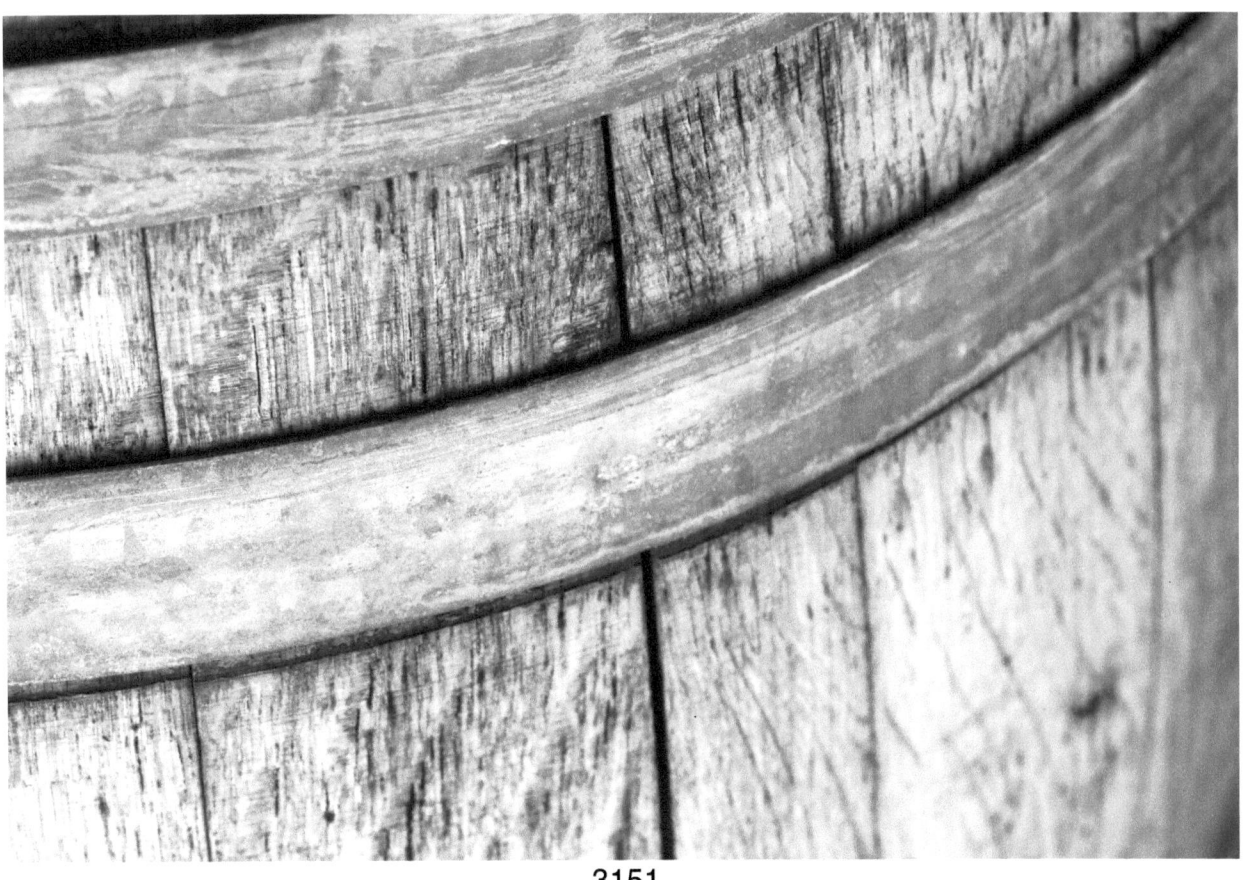

3151

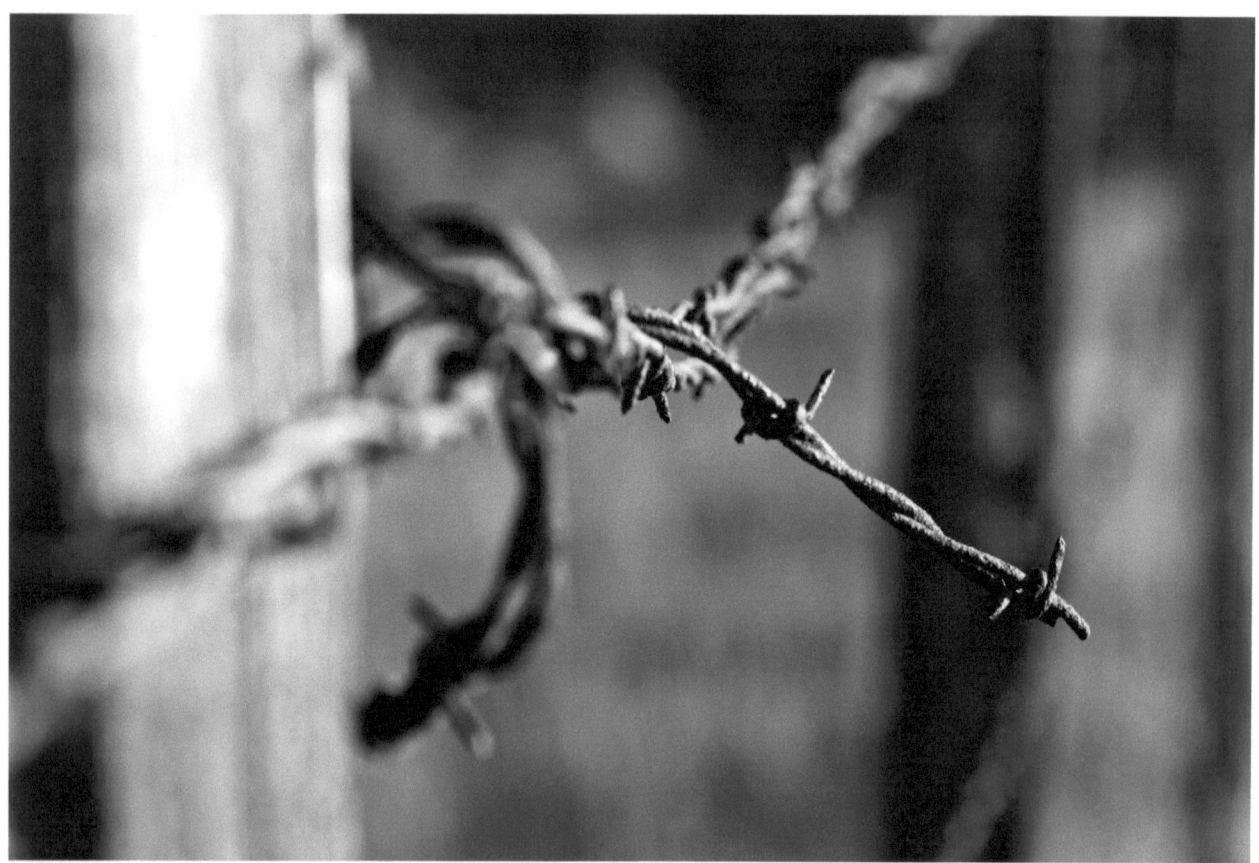

3359

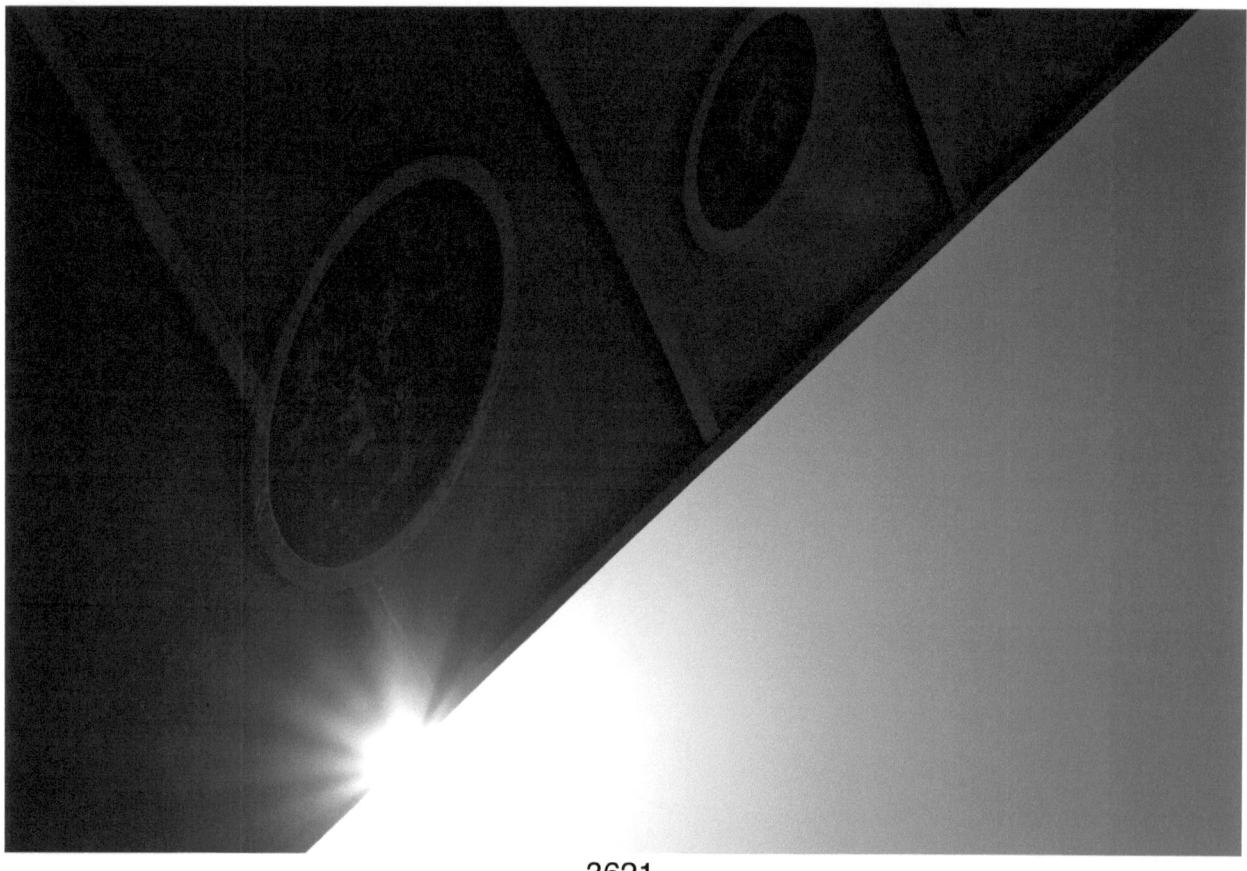

3621

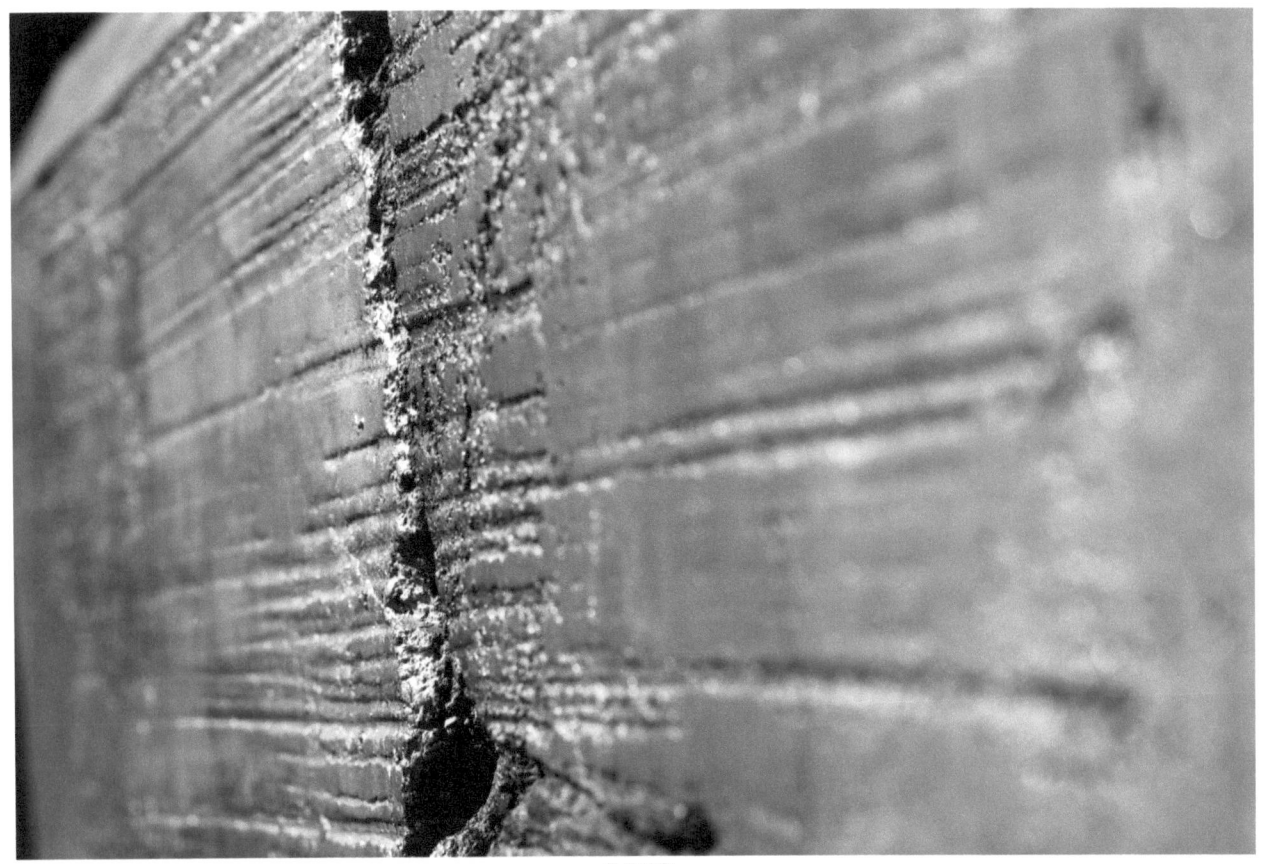

3656

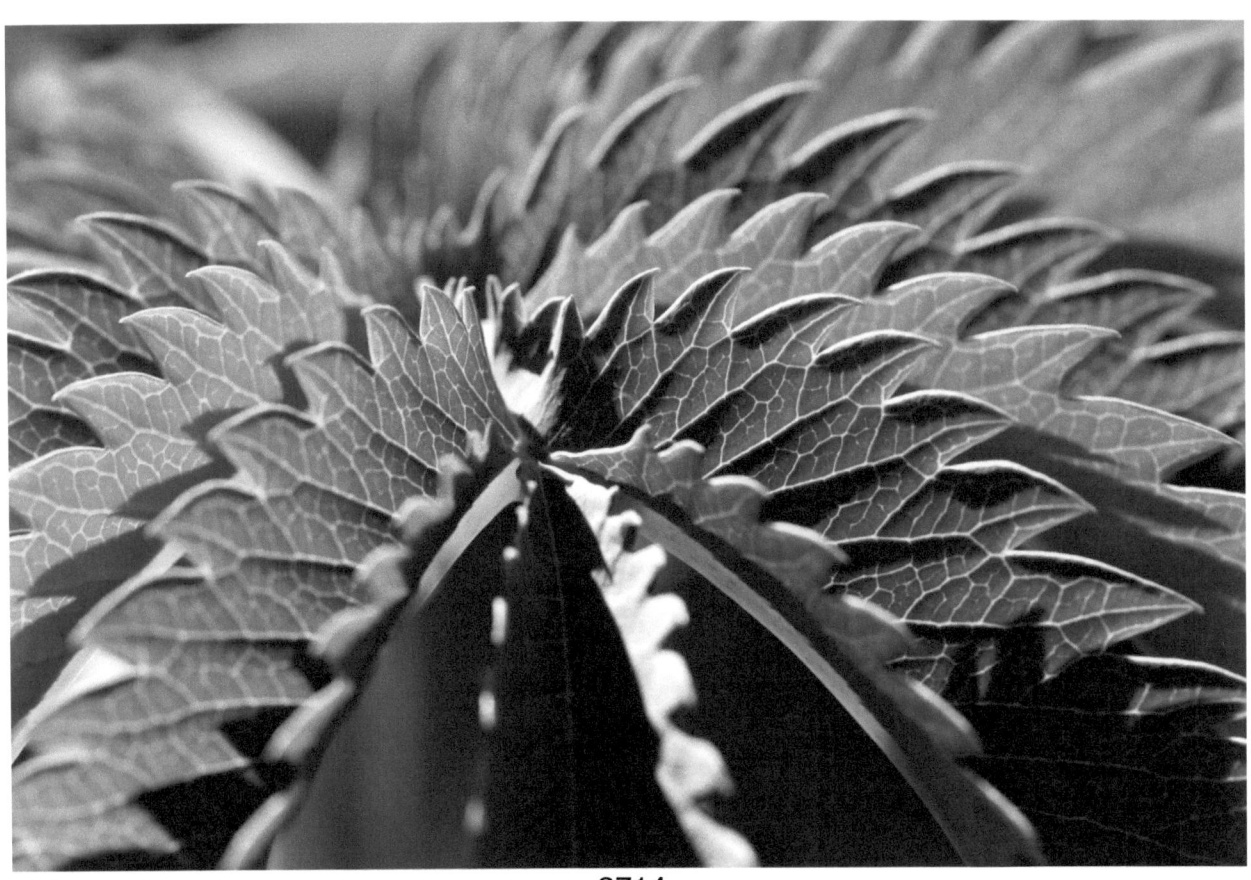

3714

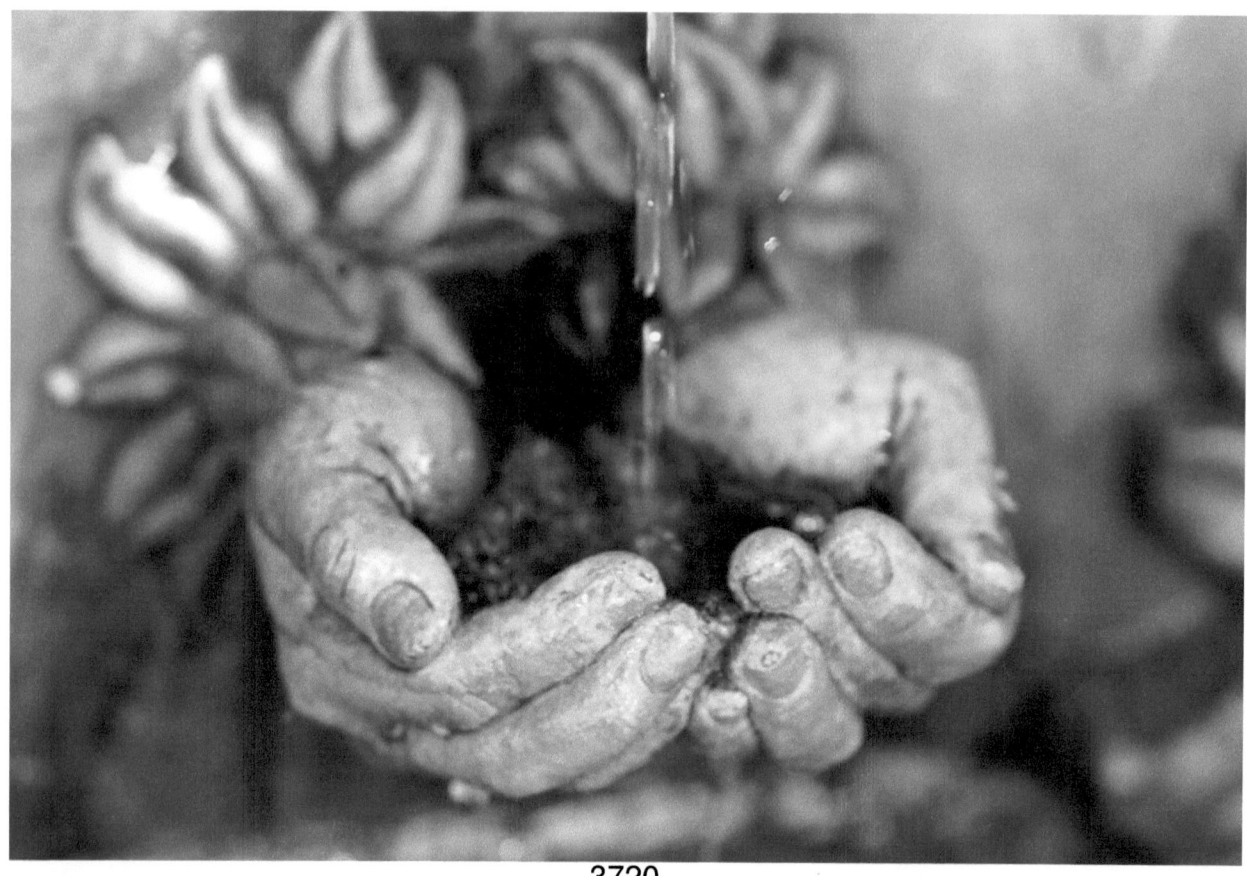

3720

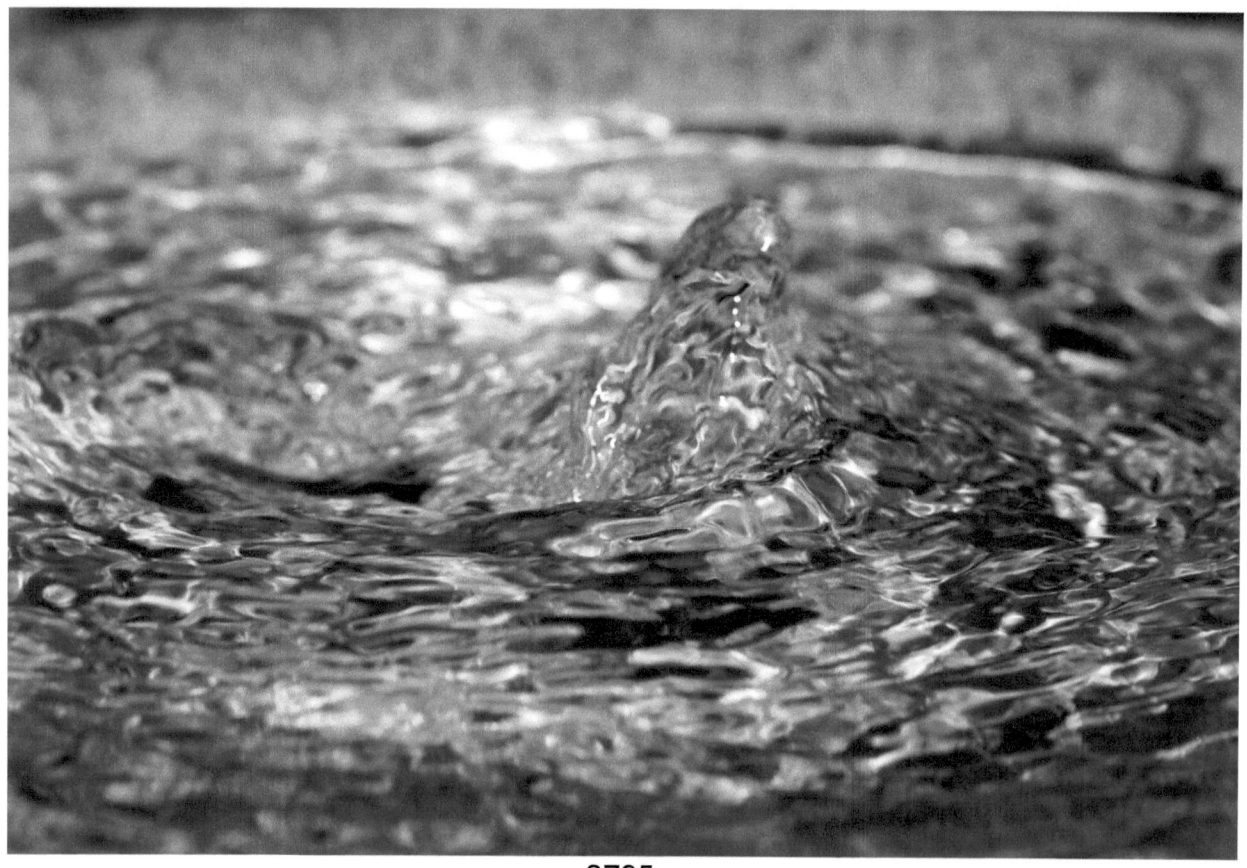

3795

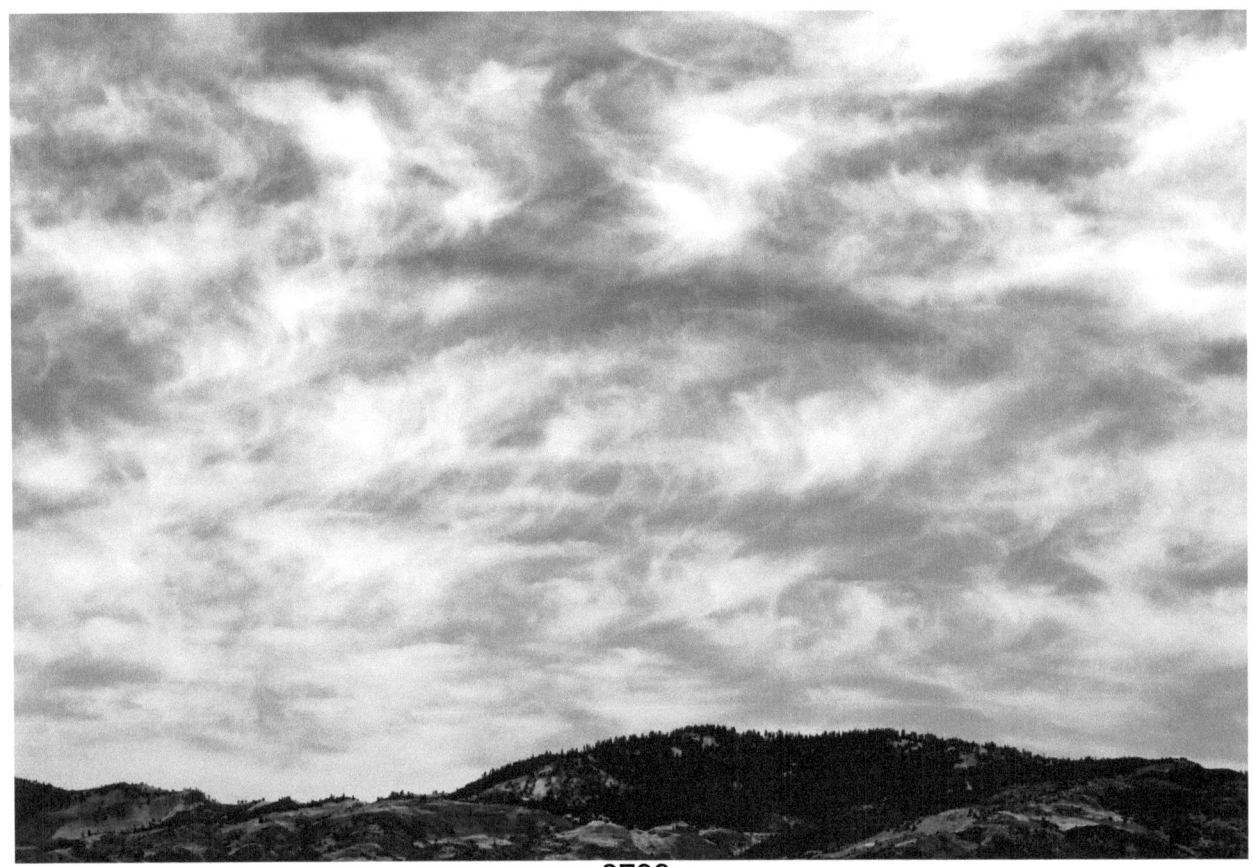

3799

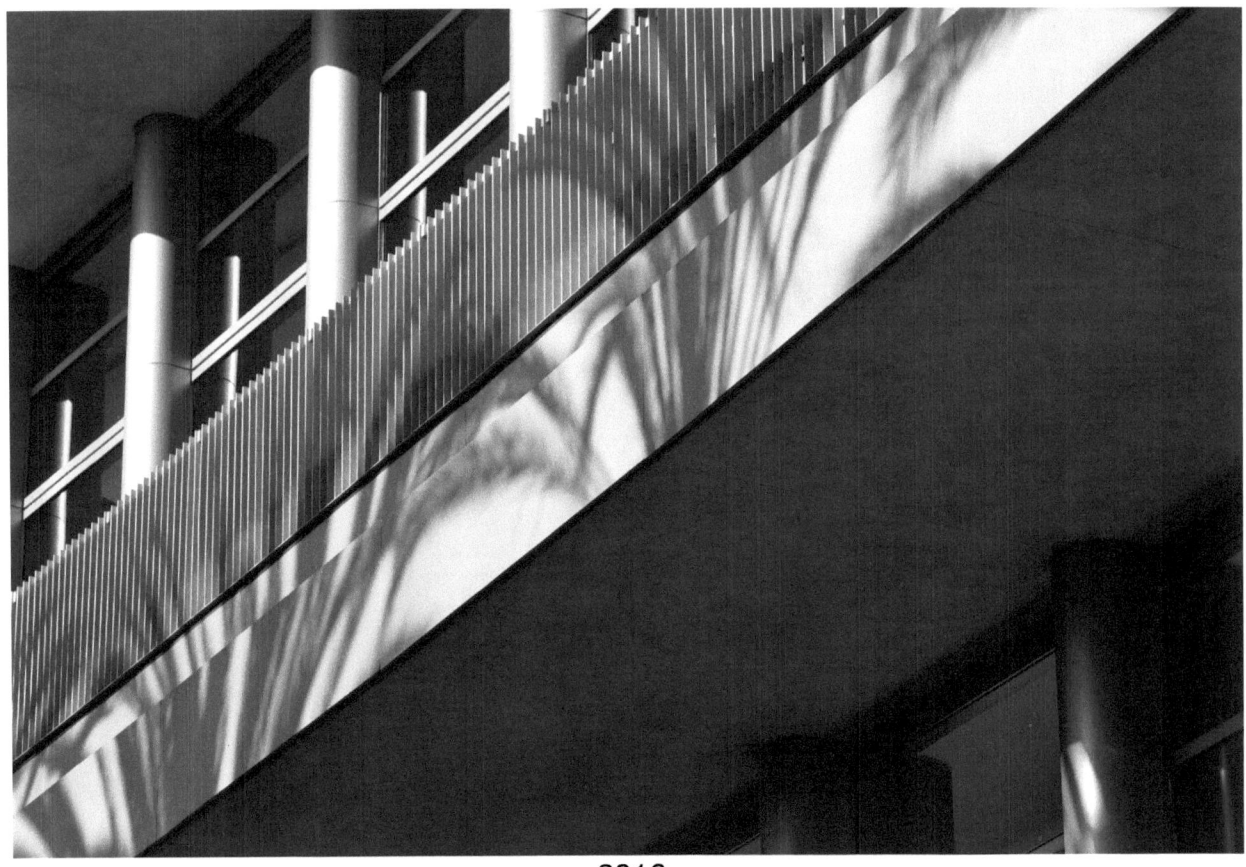

3916

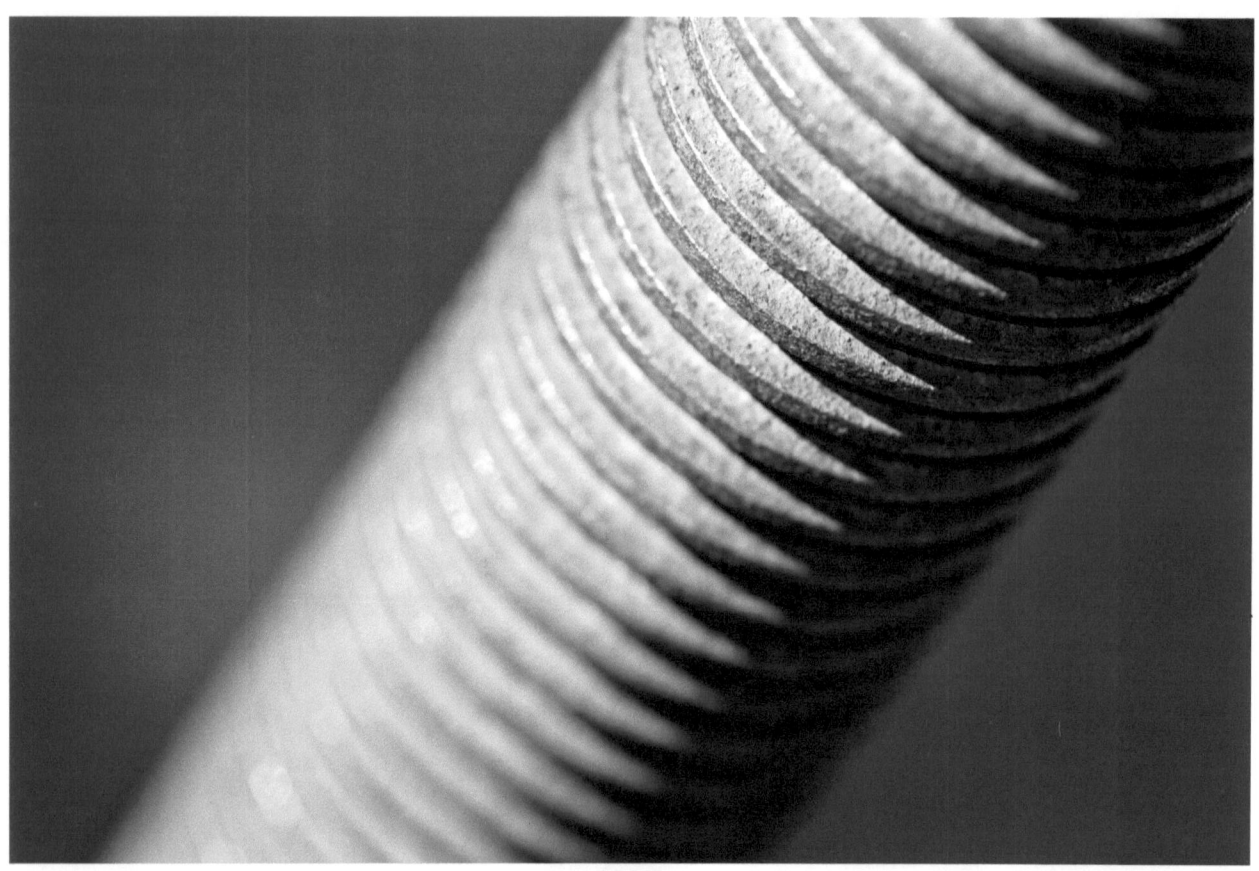

3937

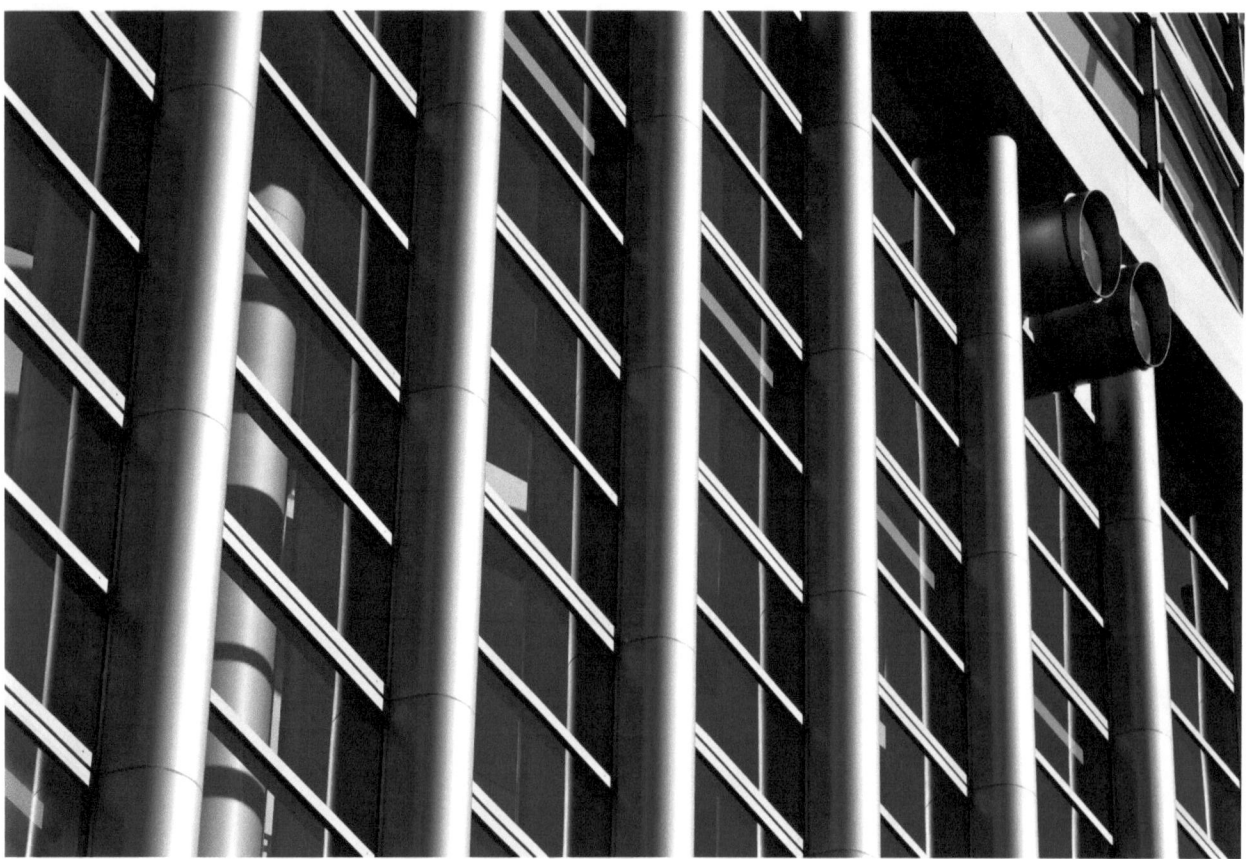

3943

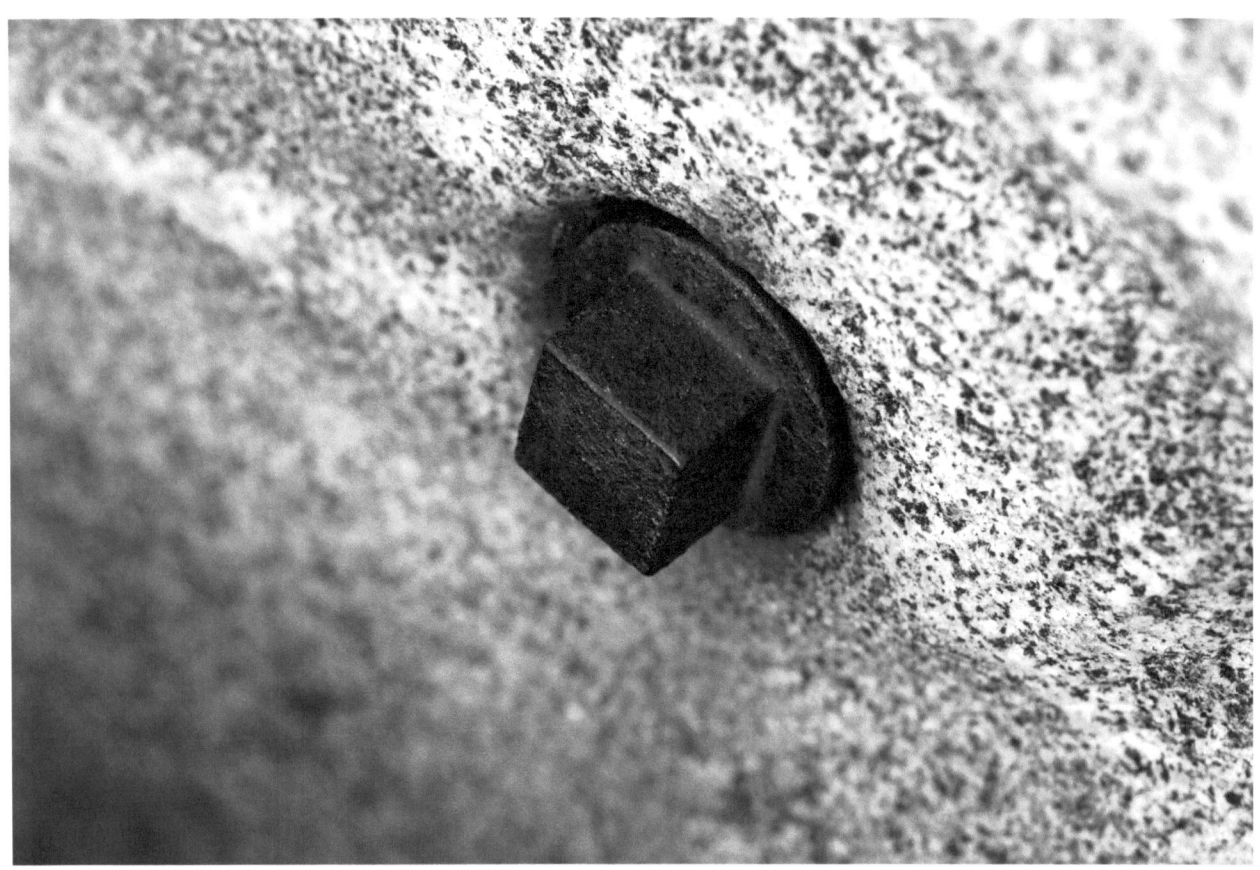

4035

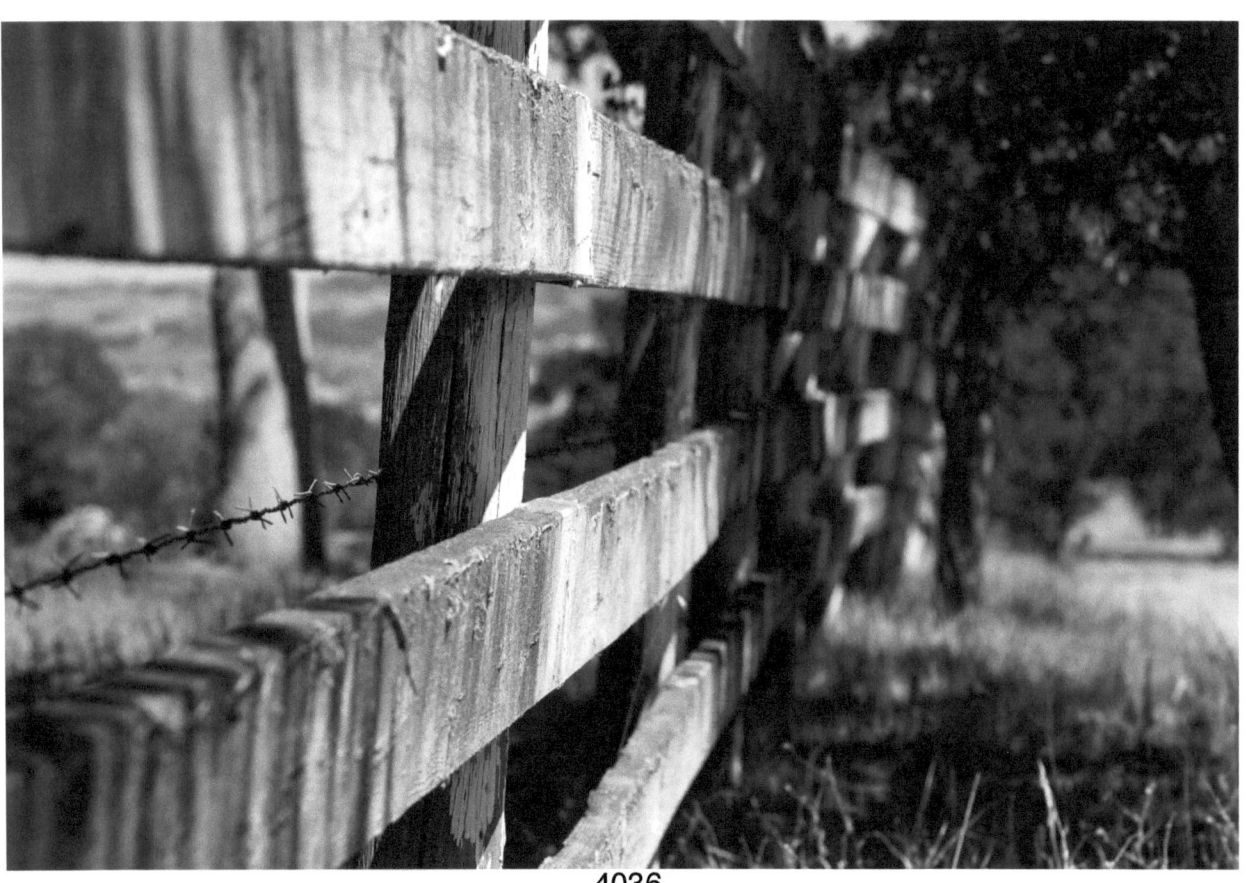

4036

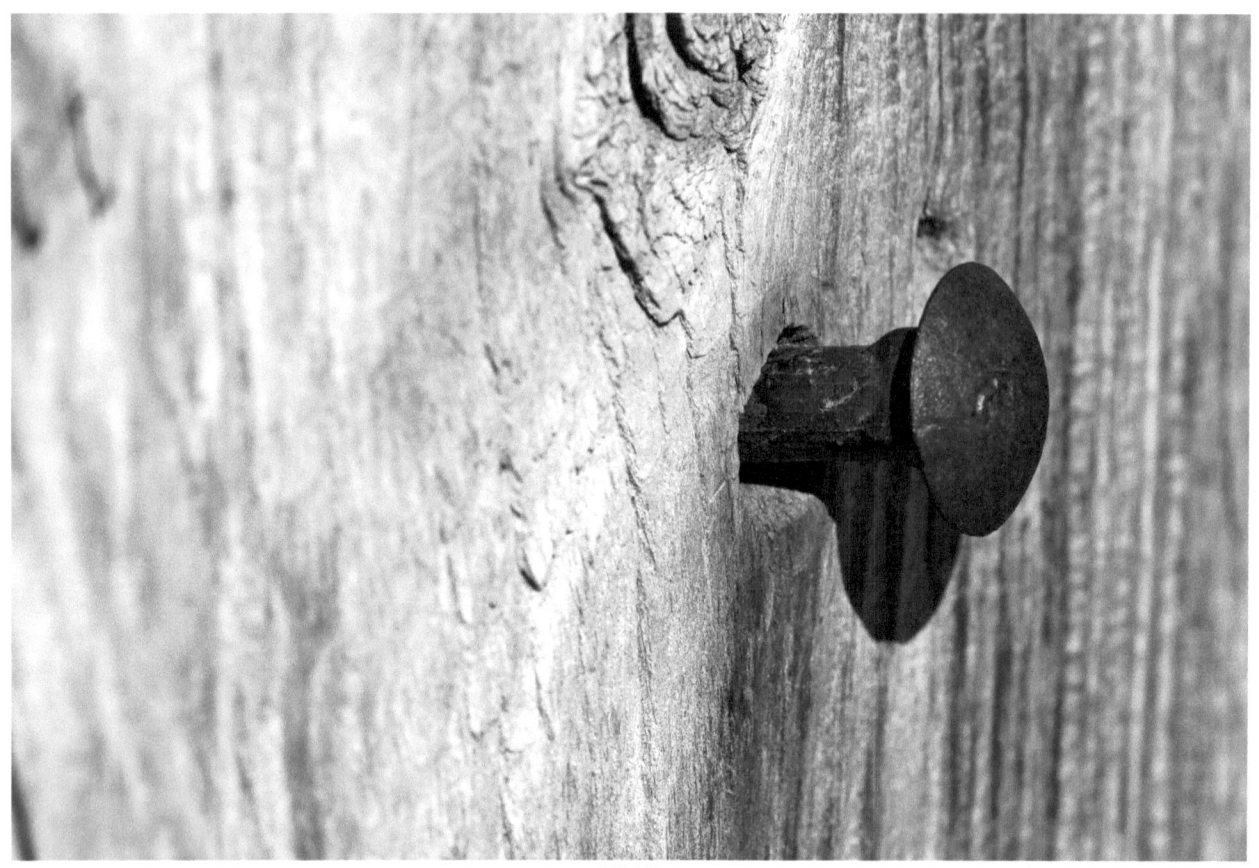

4043

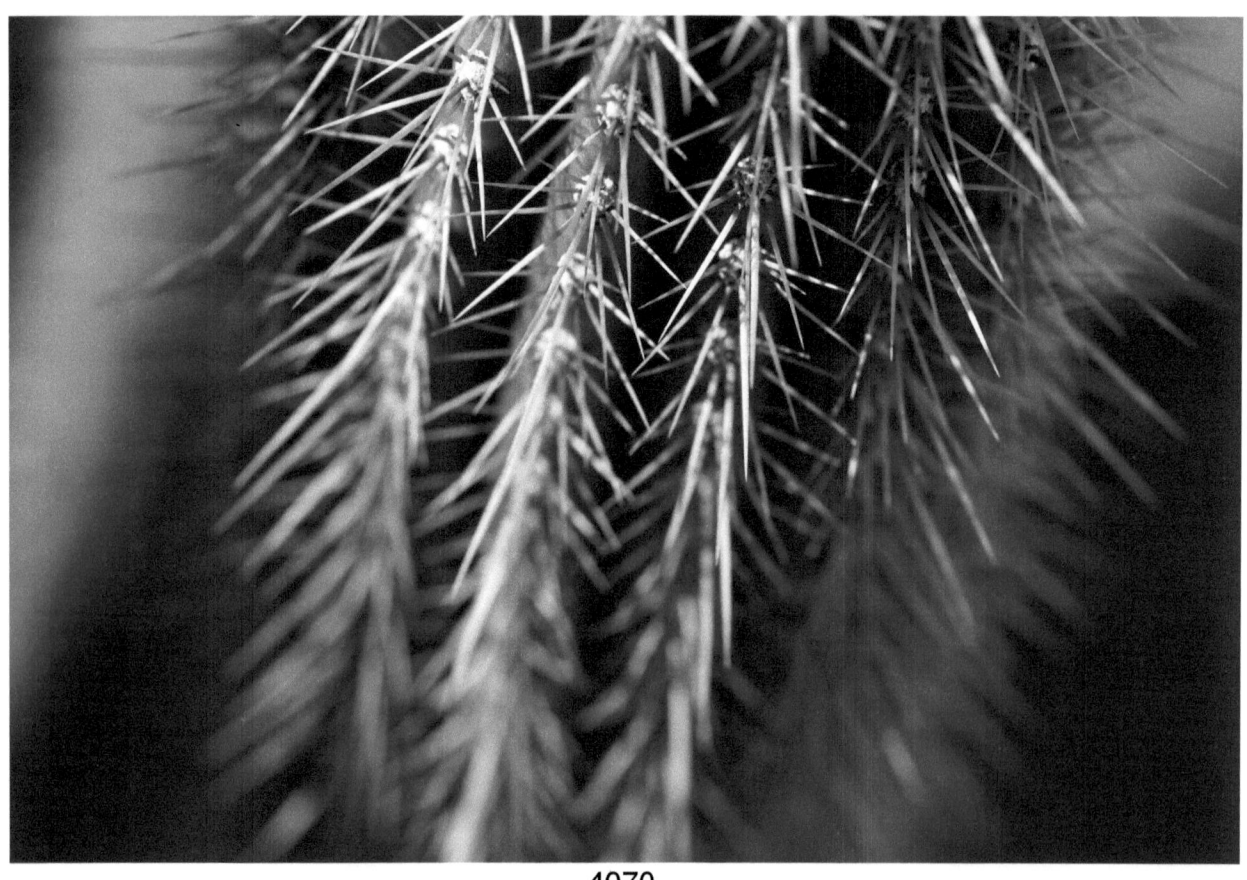

4070

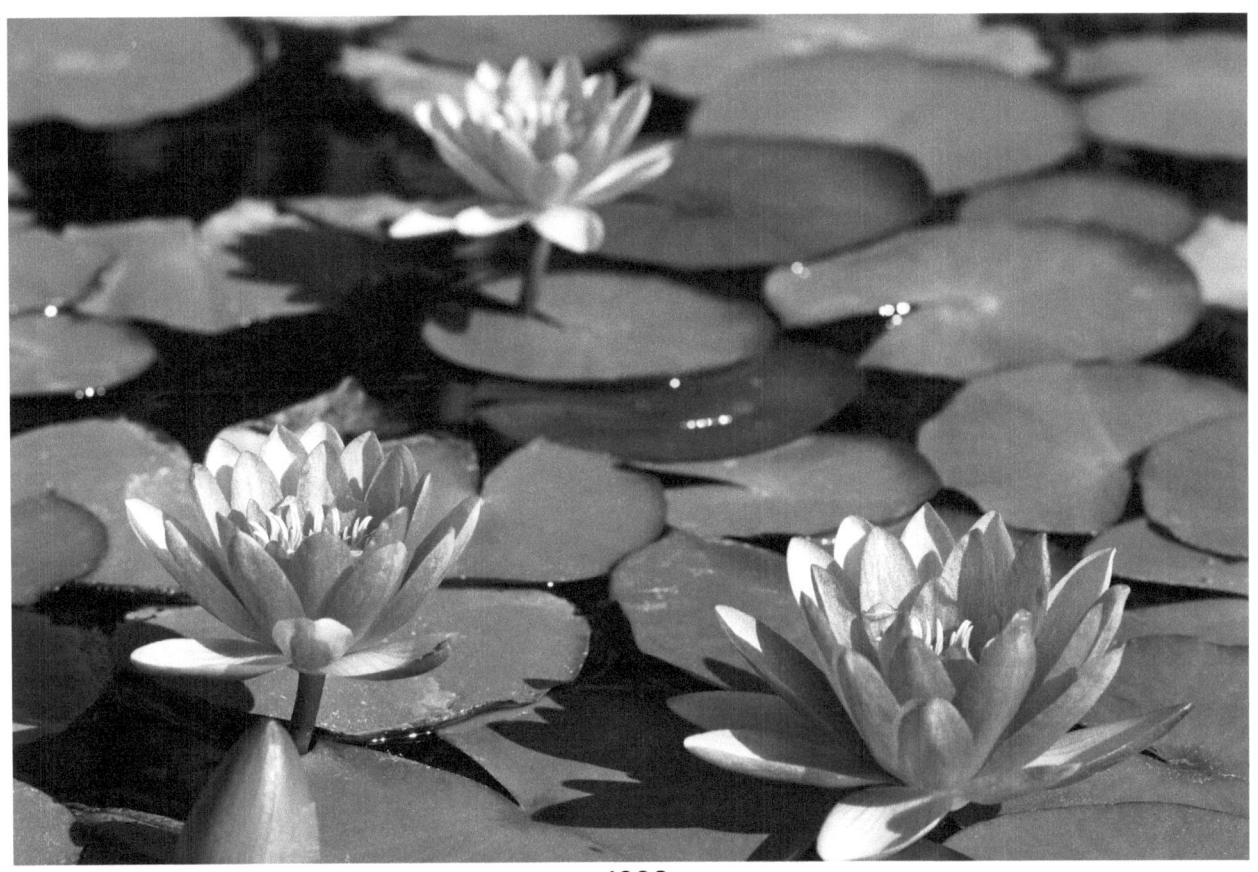

4098

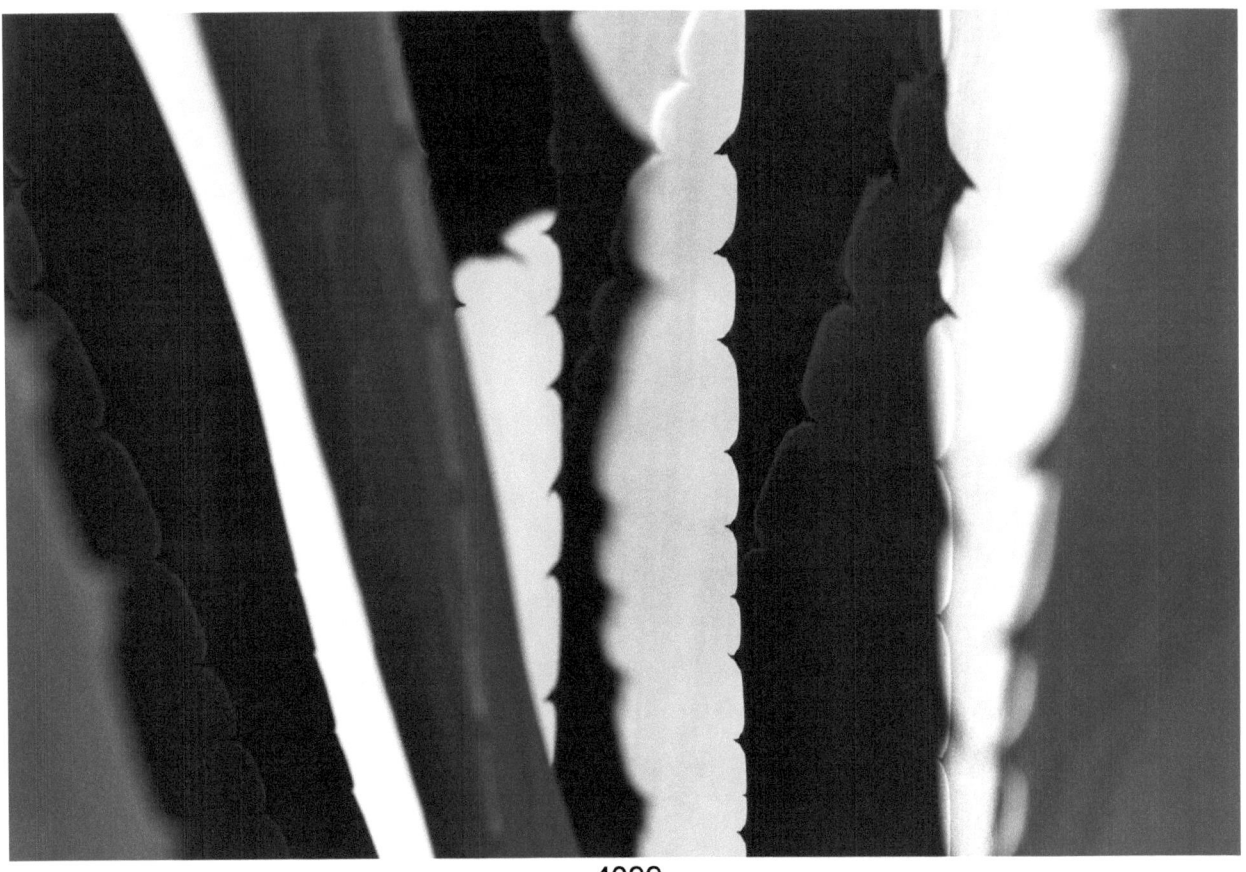

4099

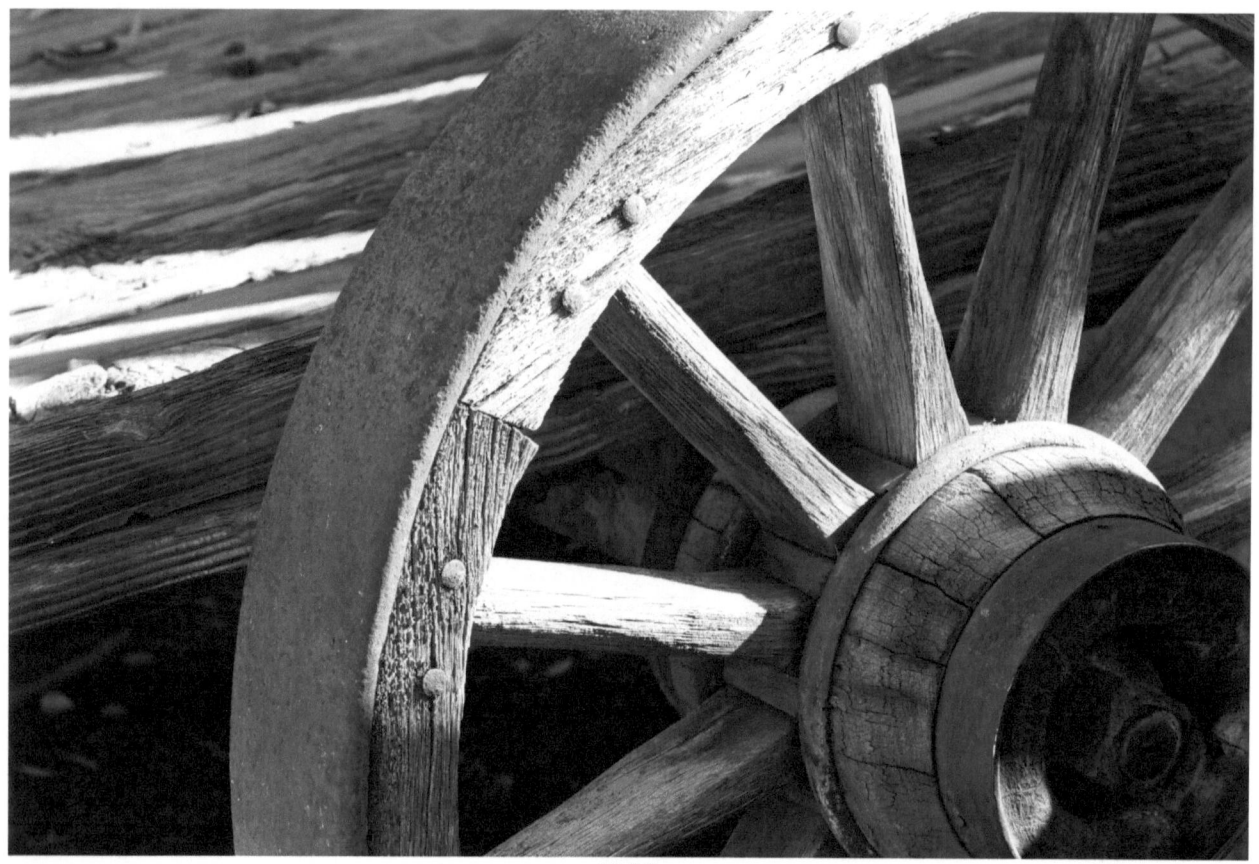

4128

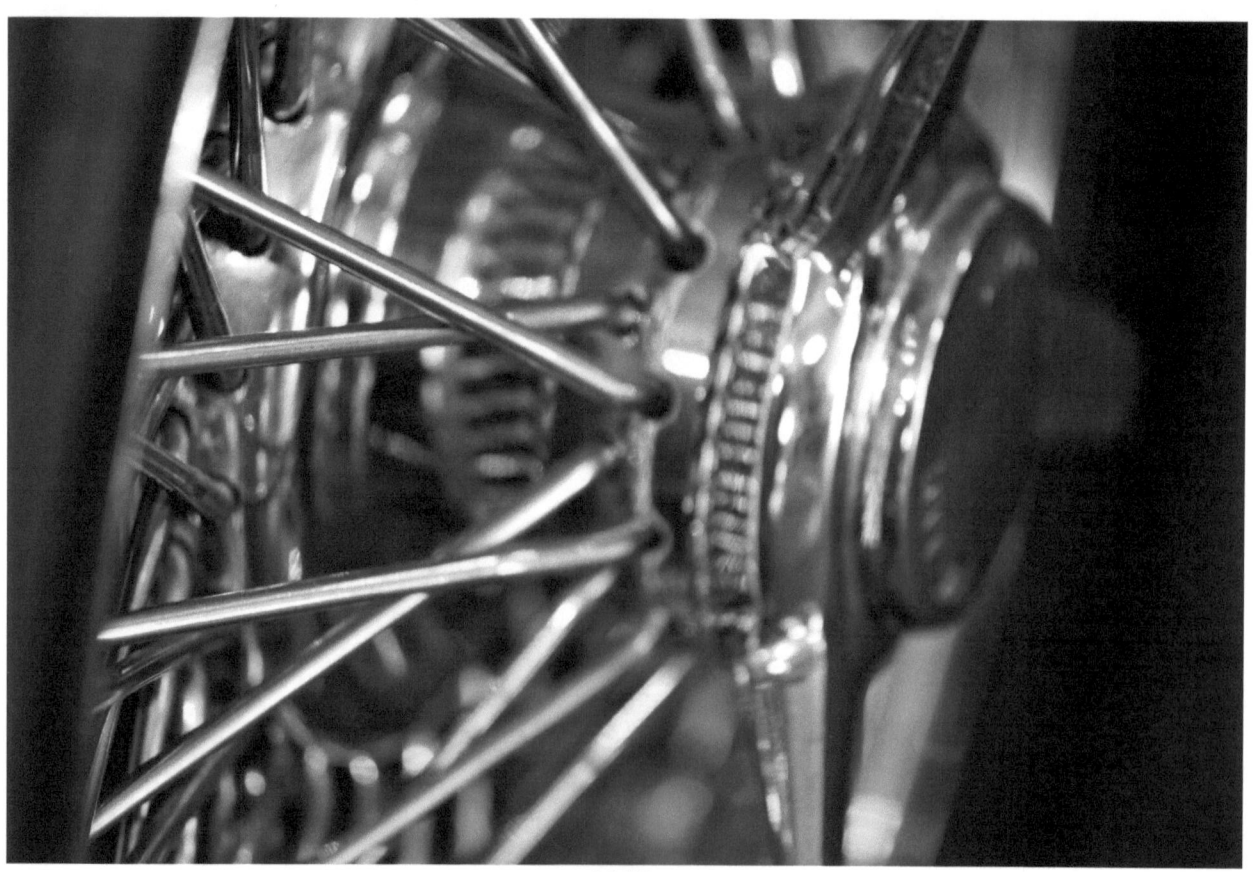

4193

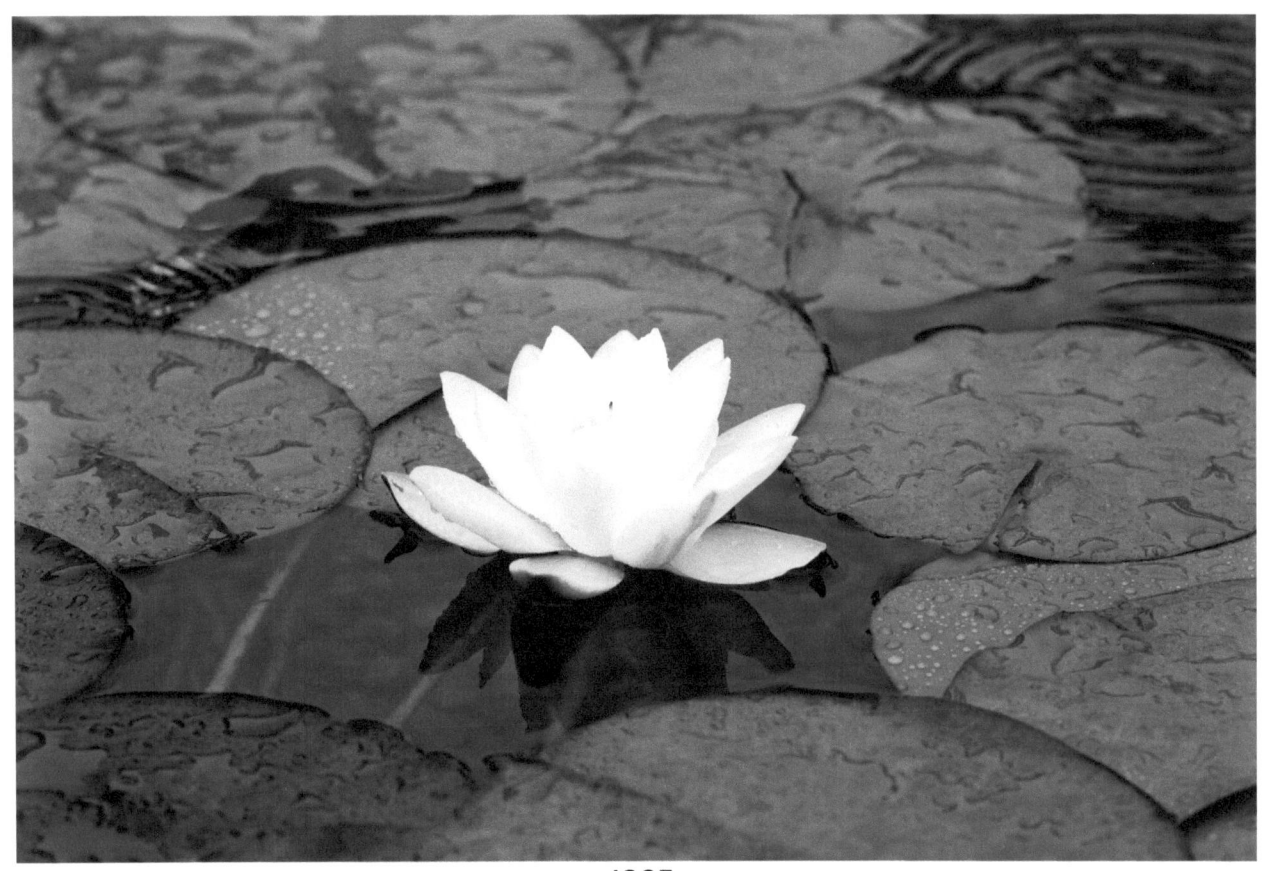

4265

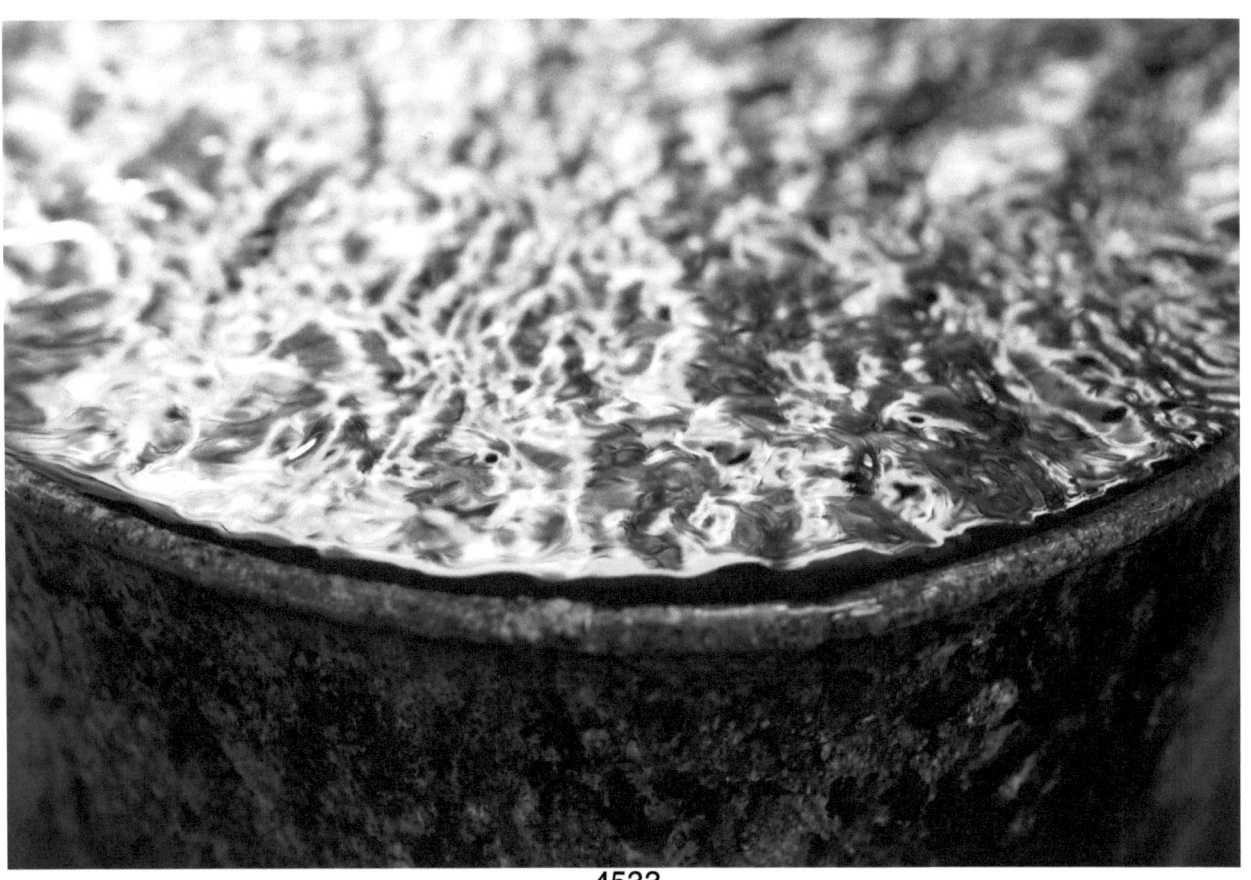

4533

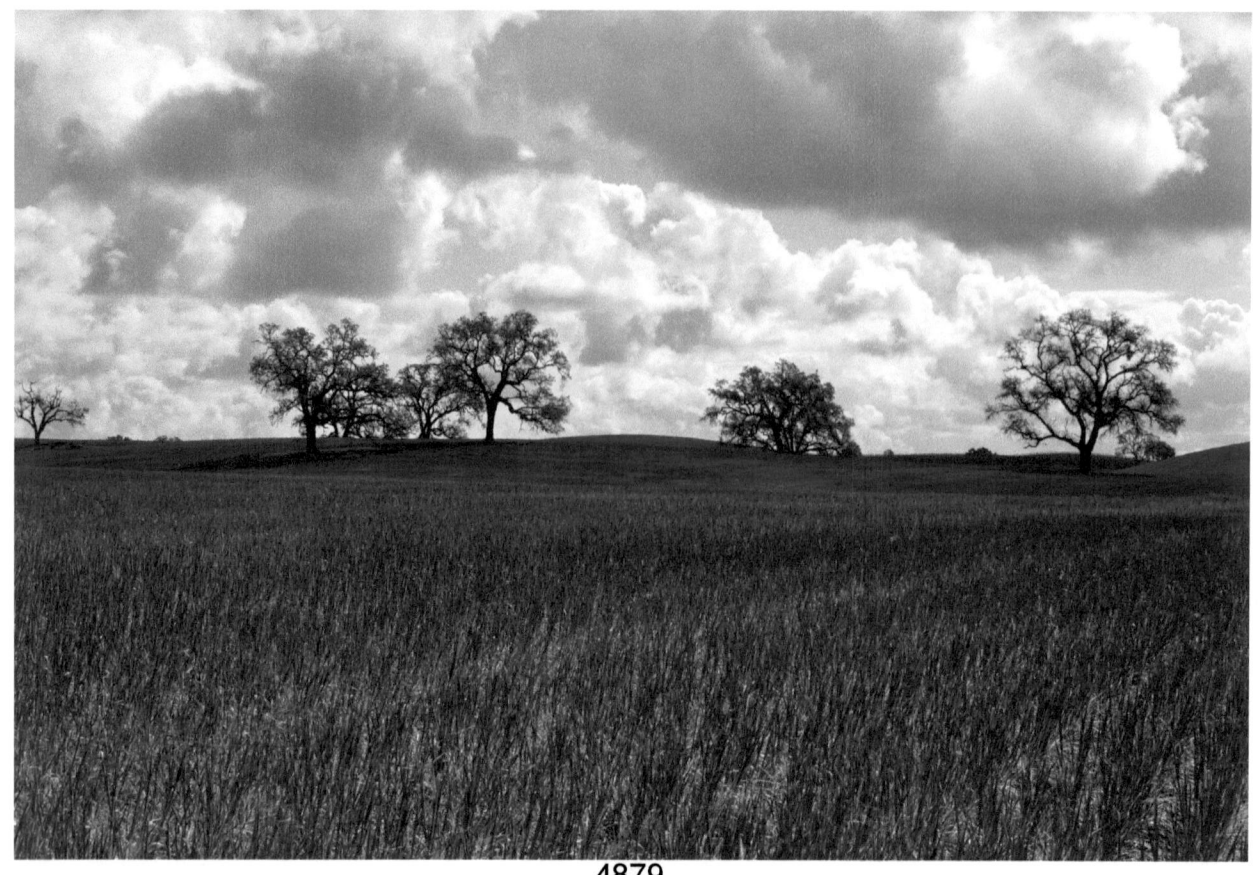

4879

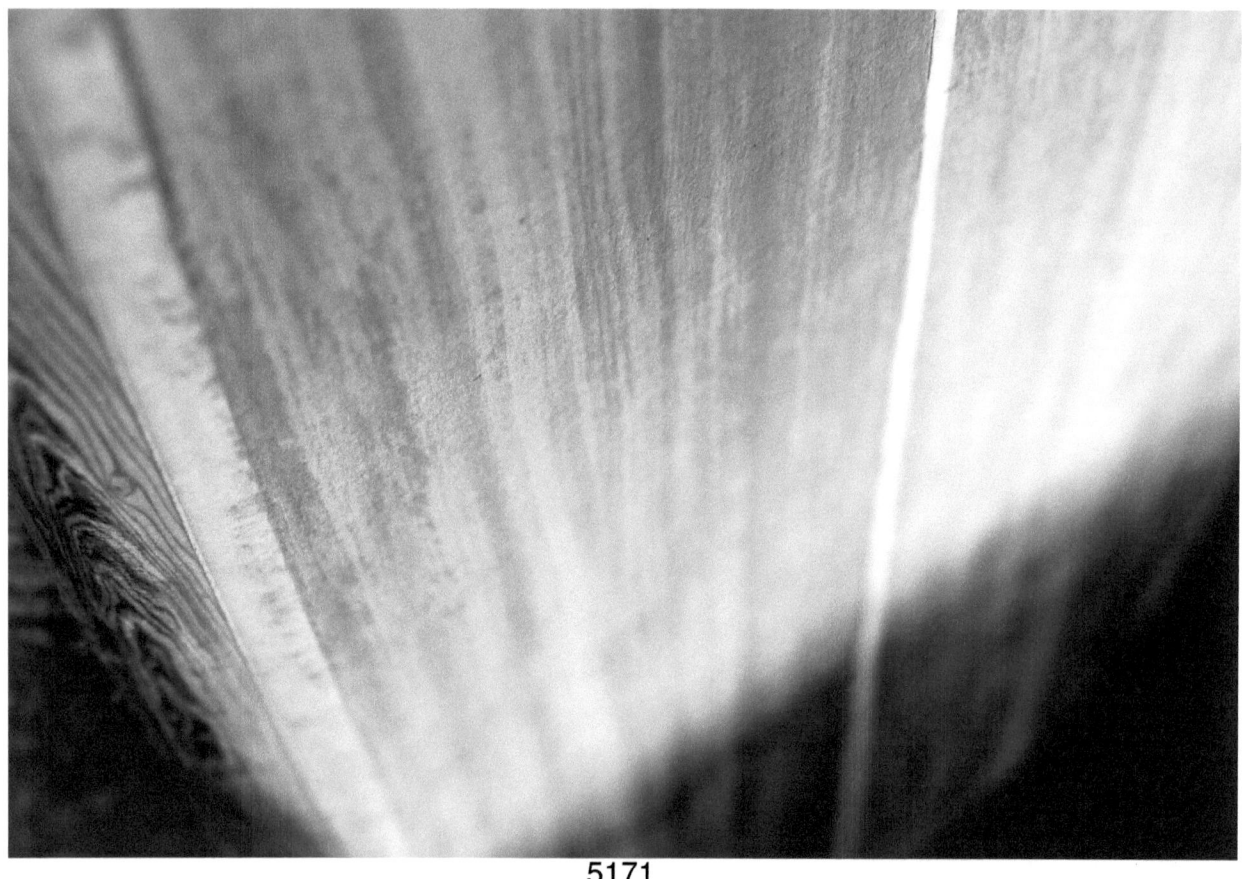

5171

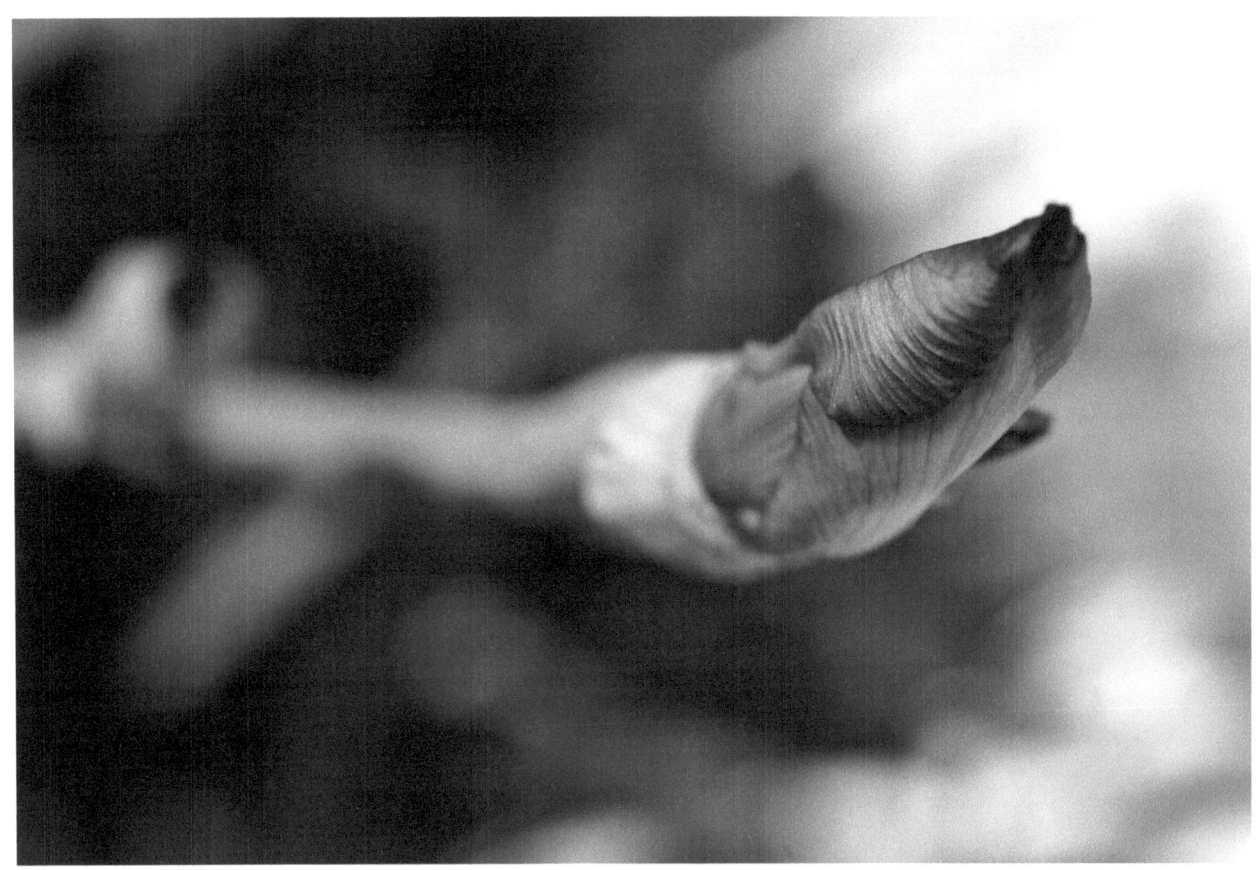

5492

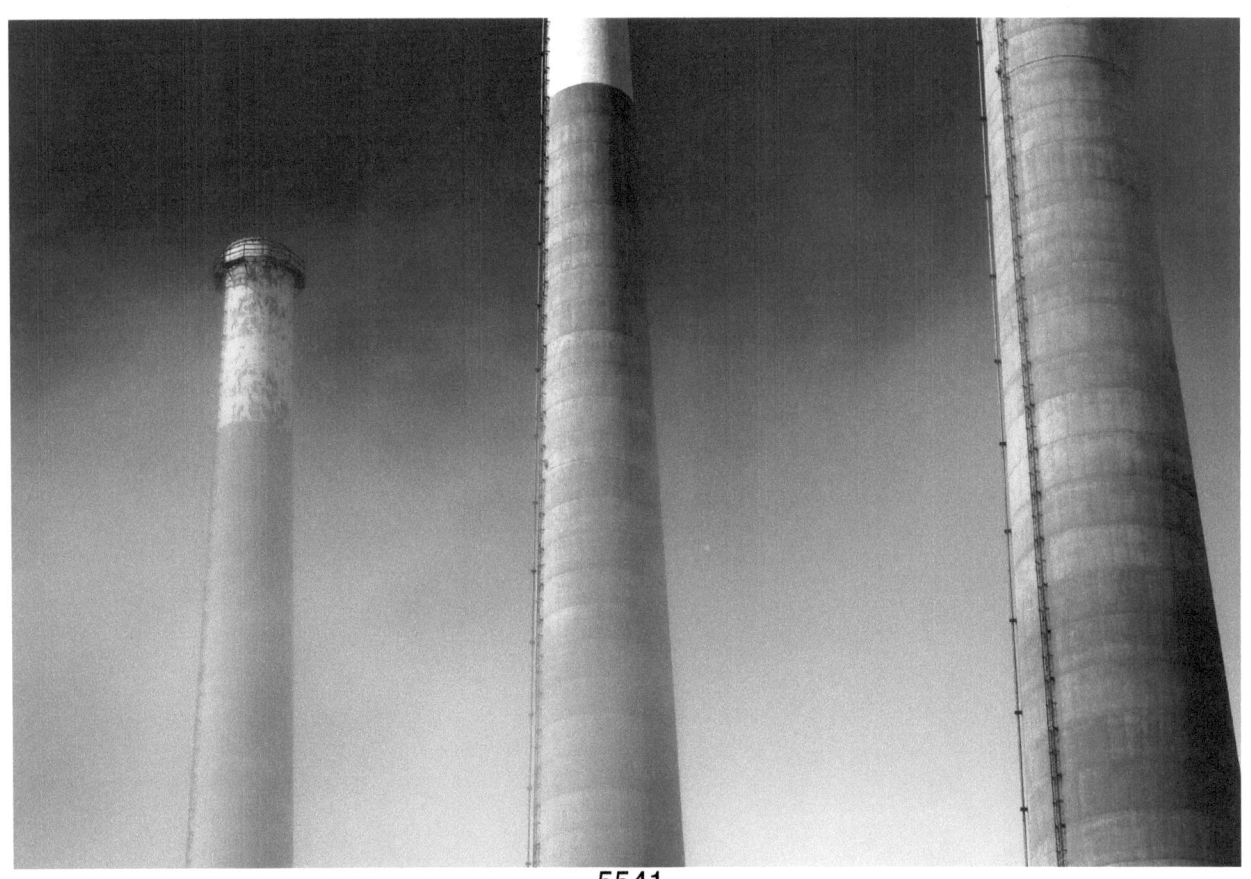

5541

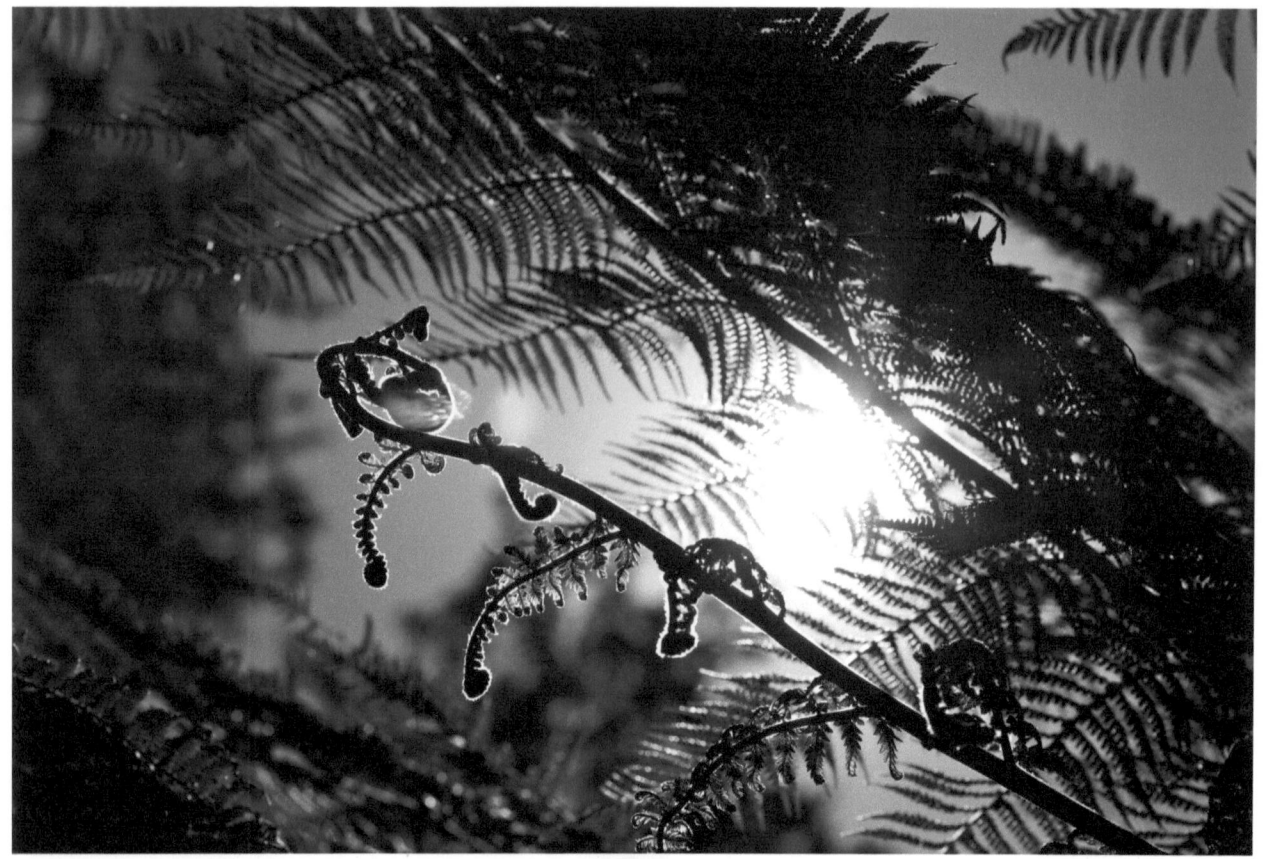

5705

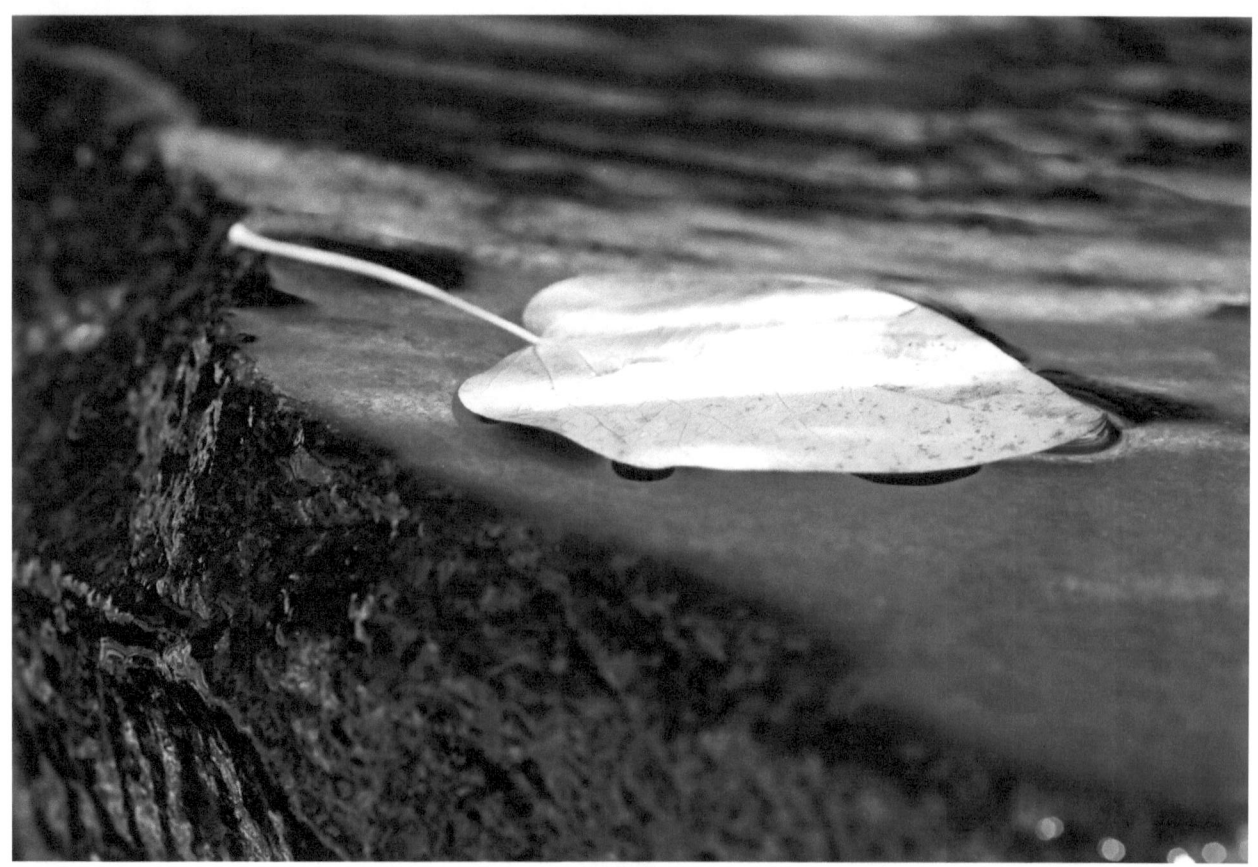

5750

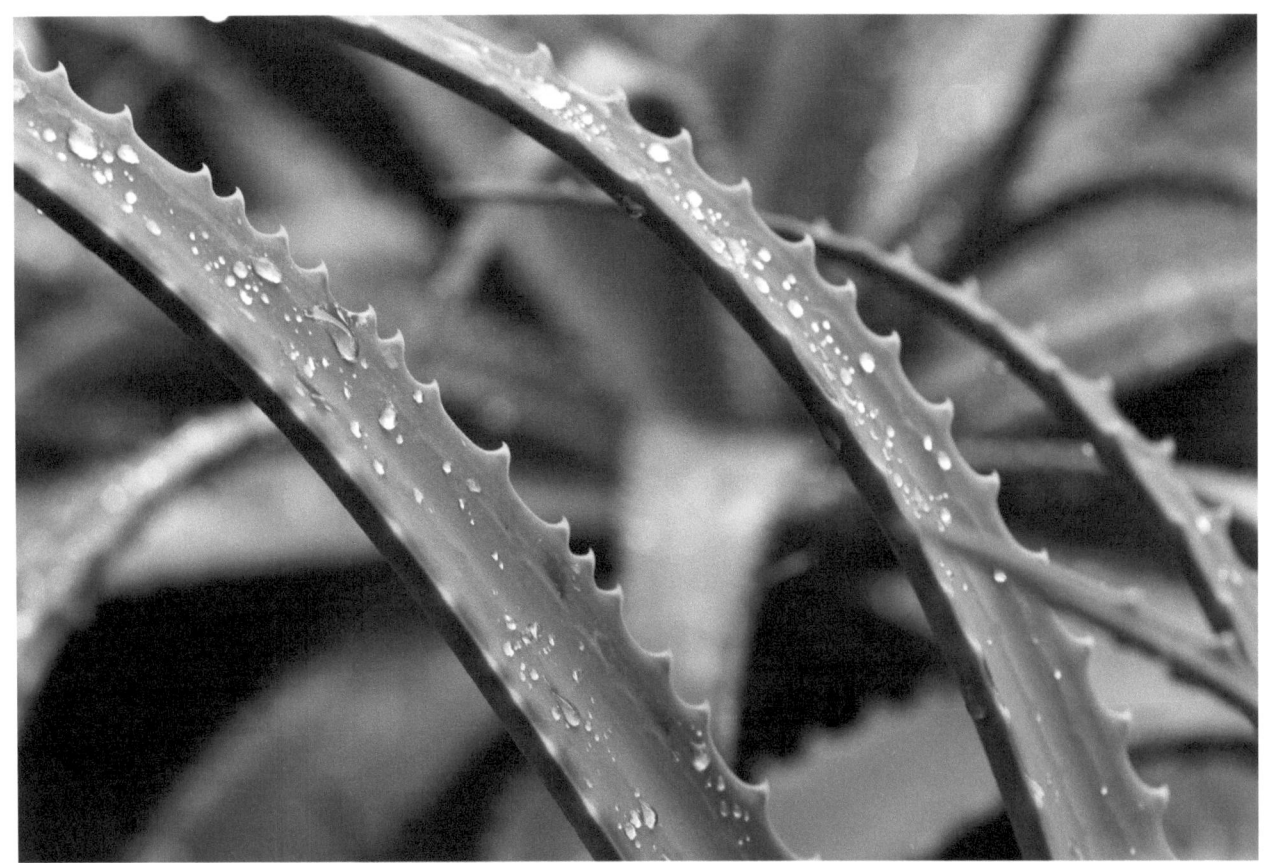

5784

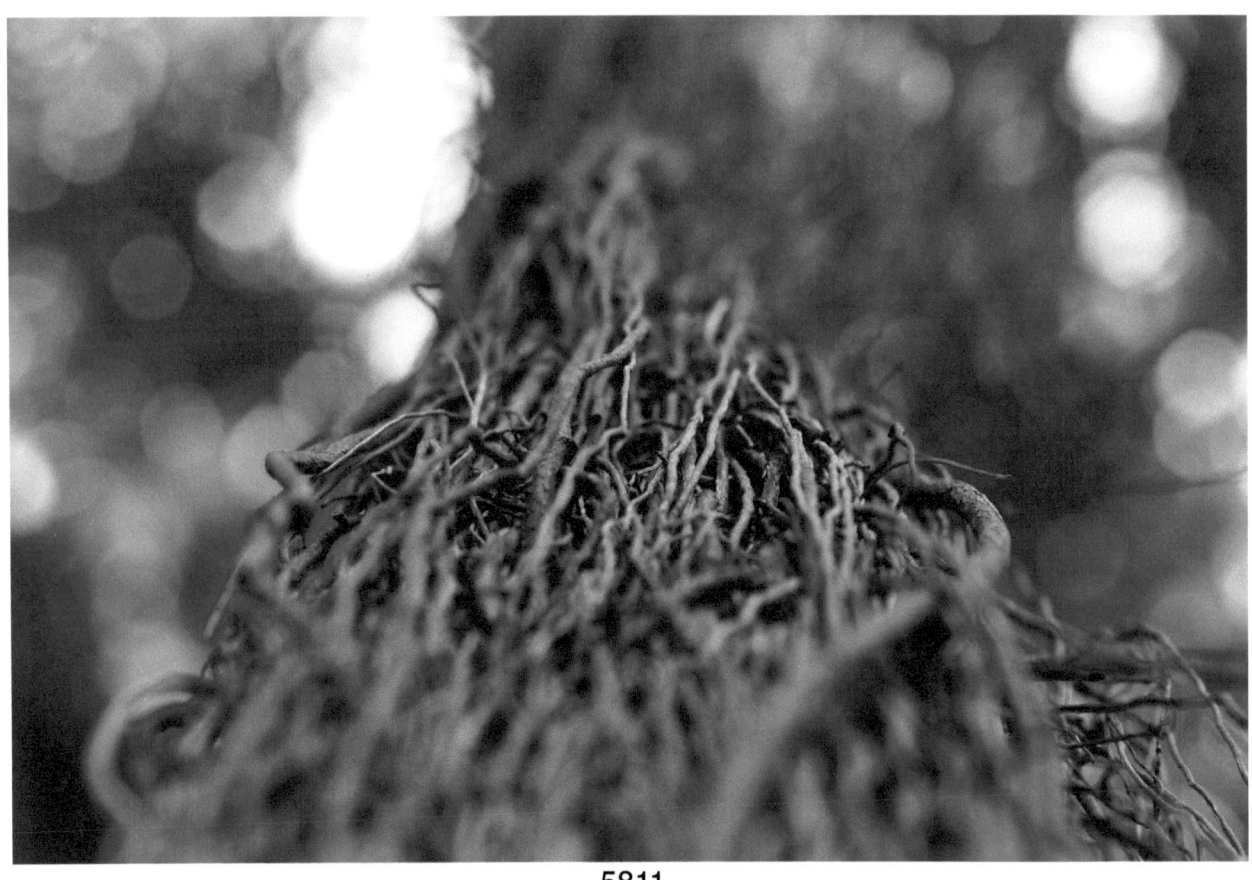

5811

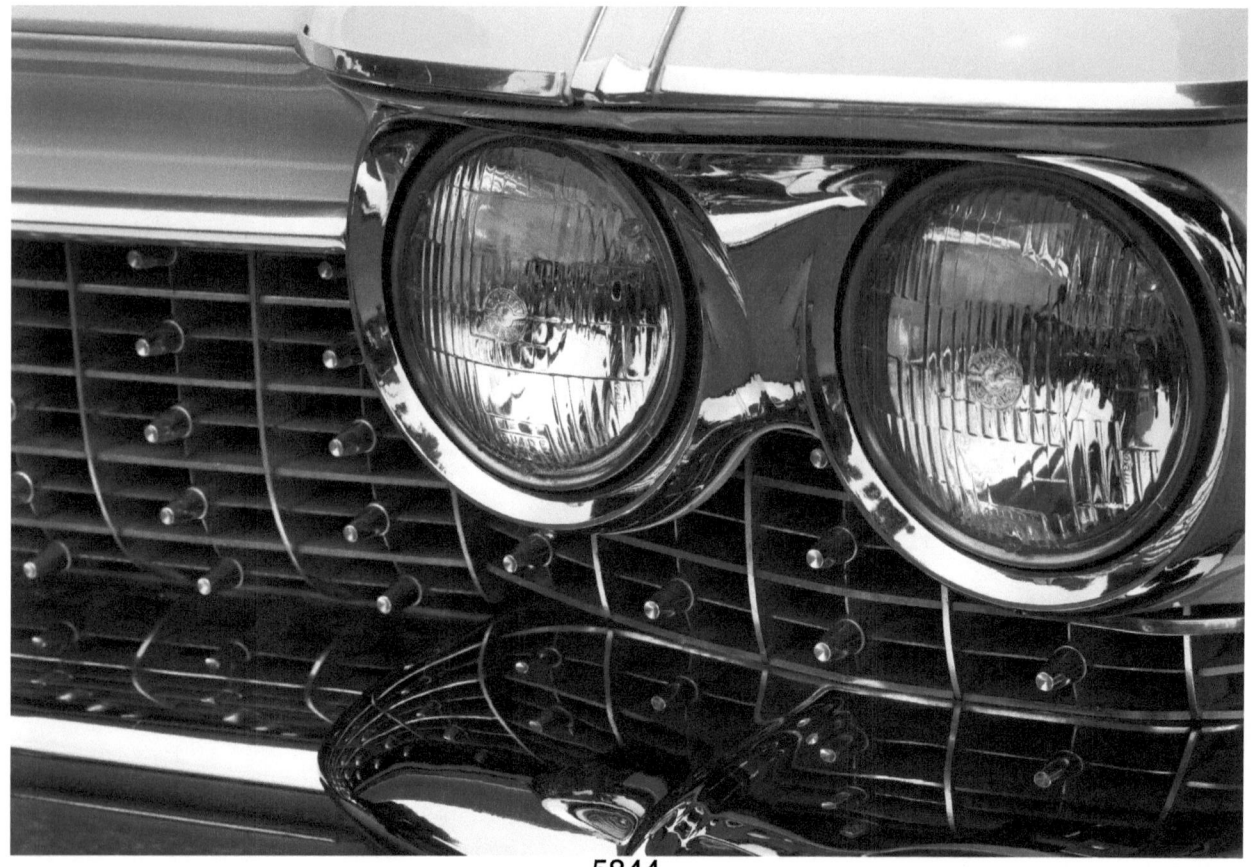

5844

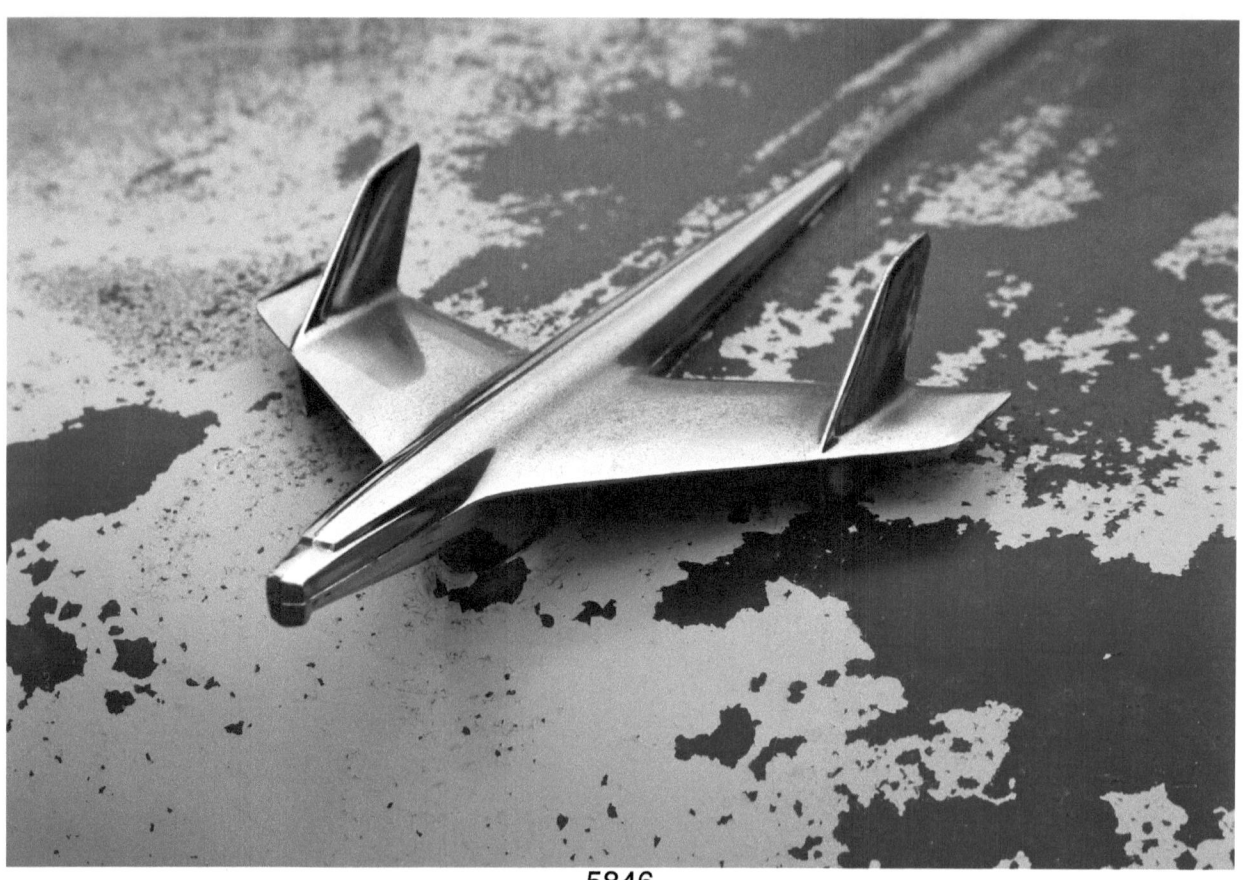

5846

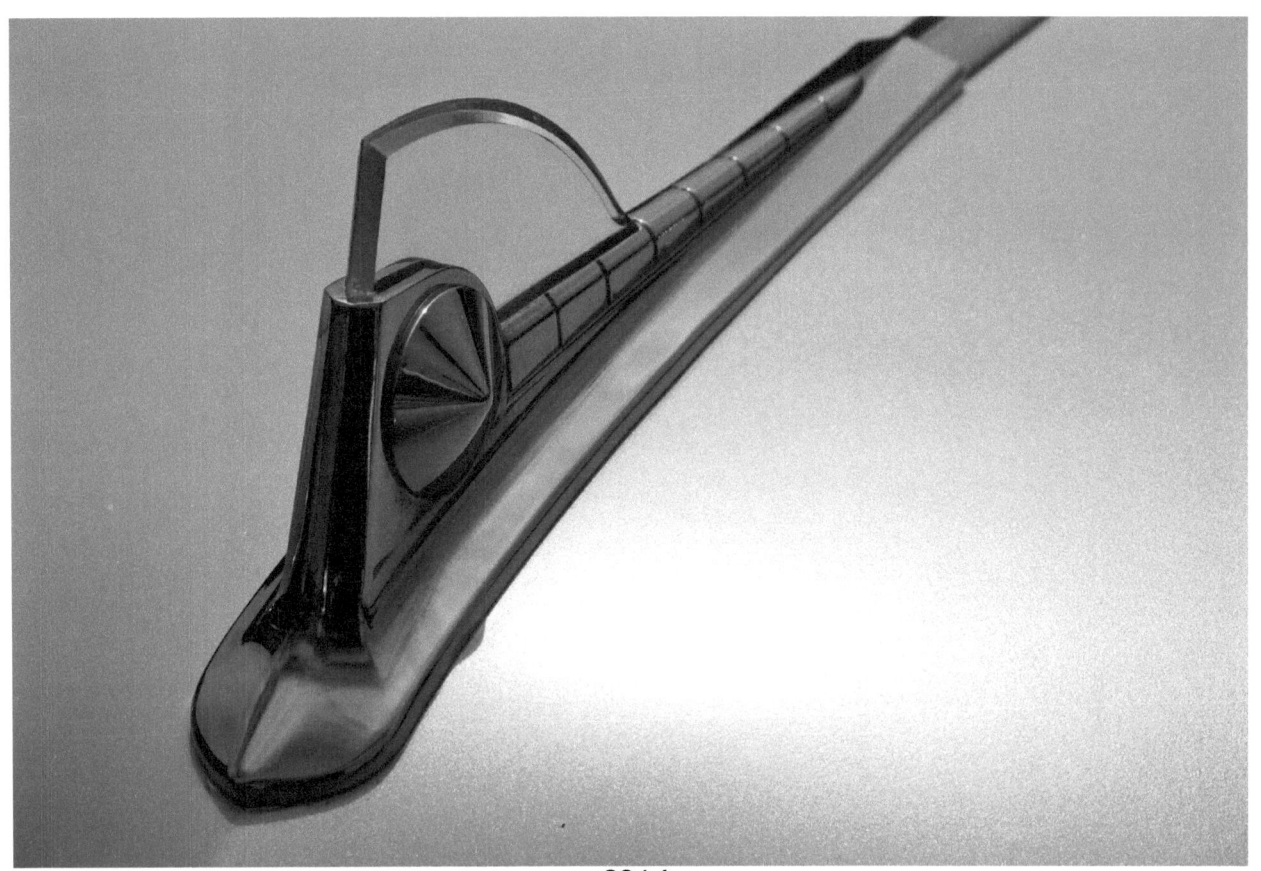

6014

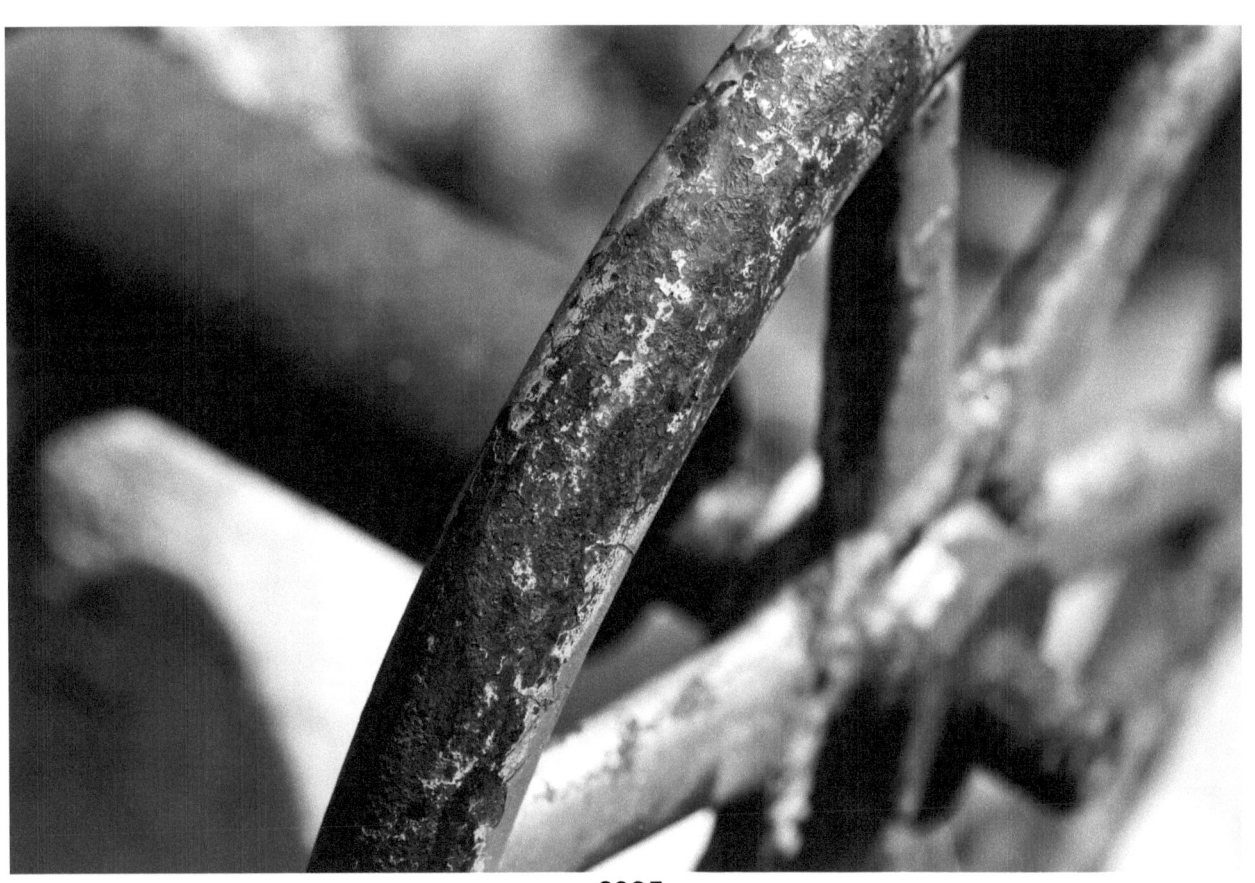

6095

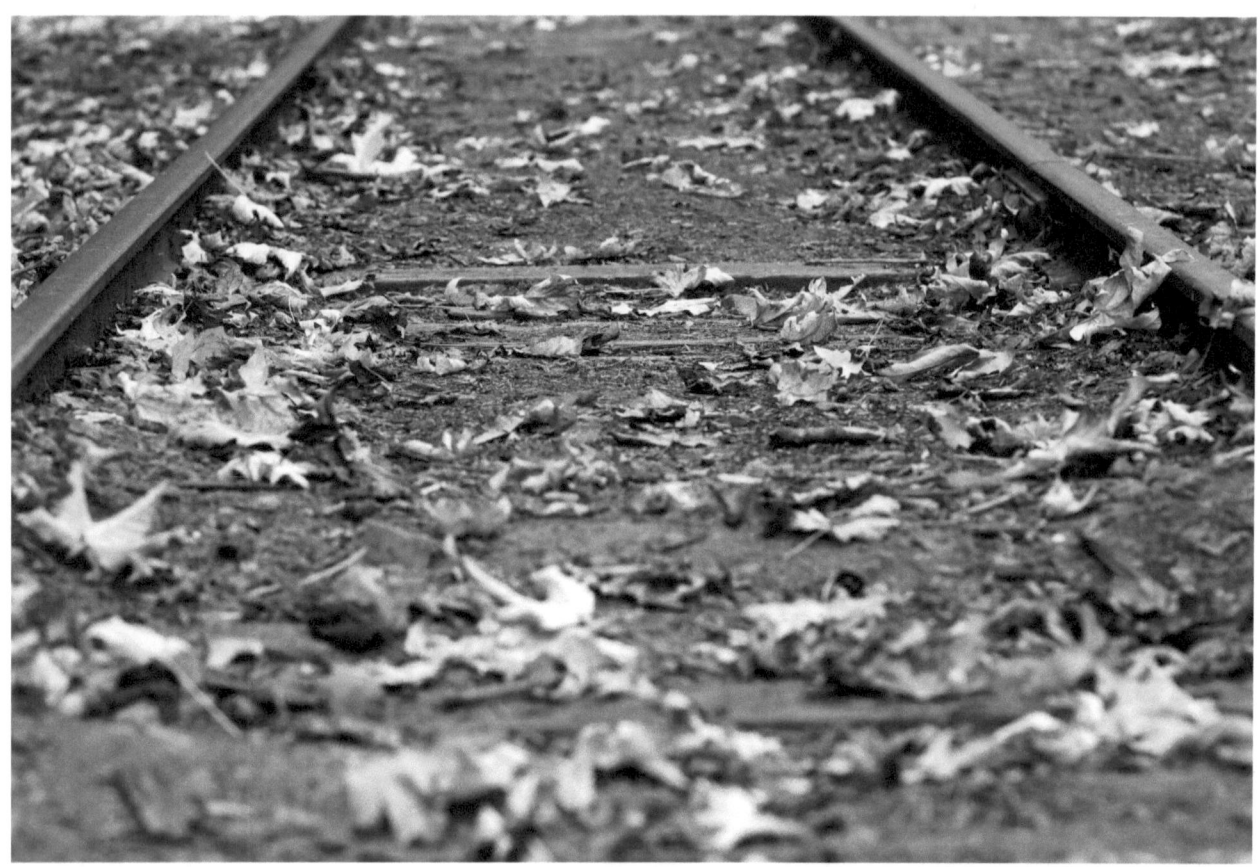

6176

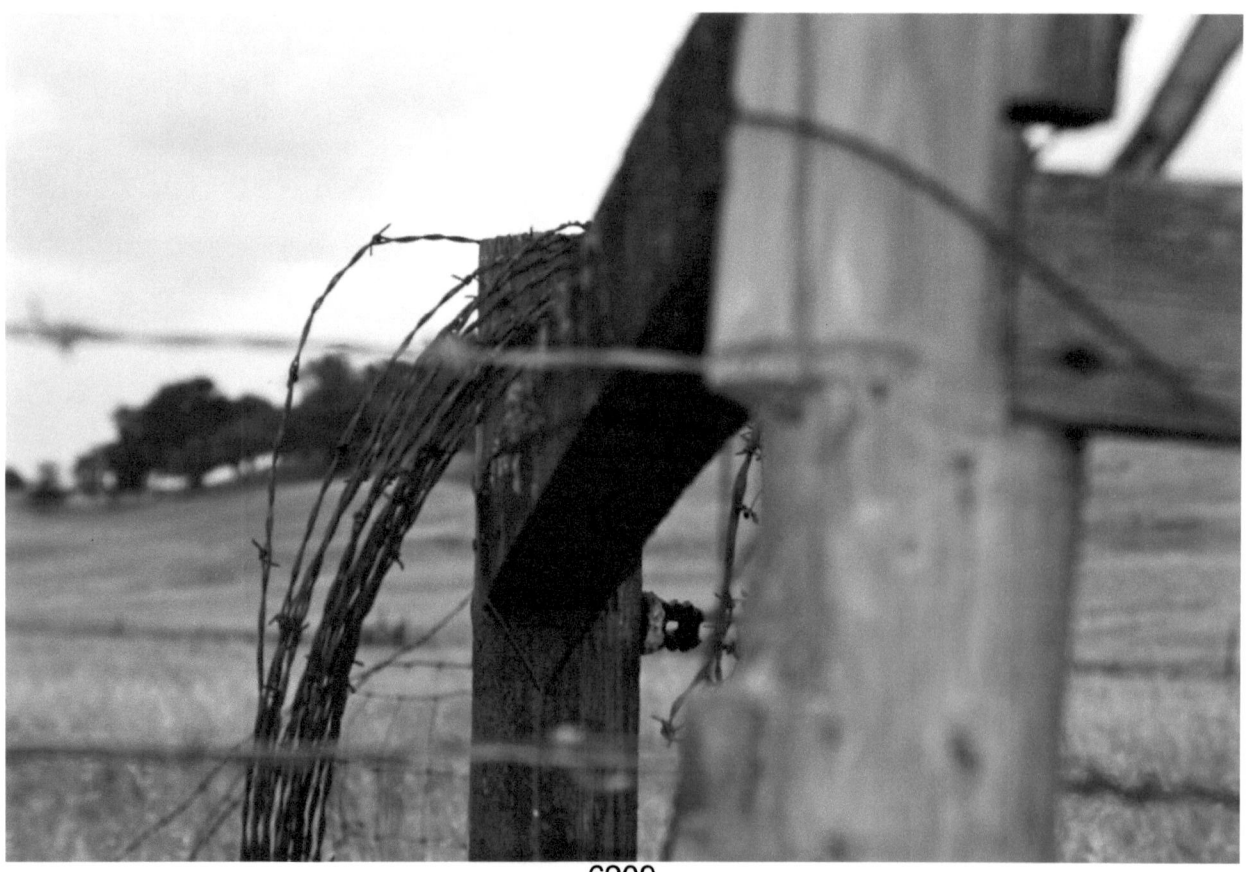

6209

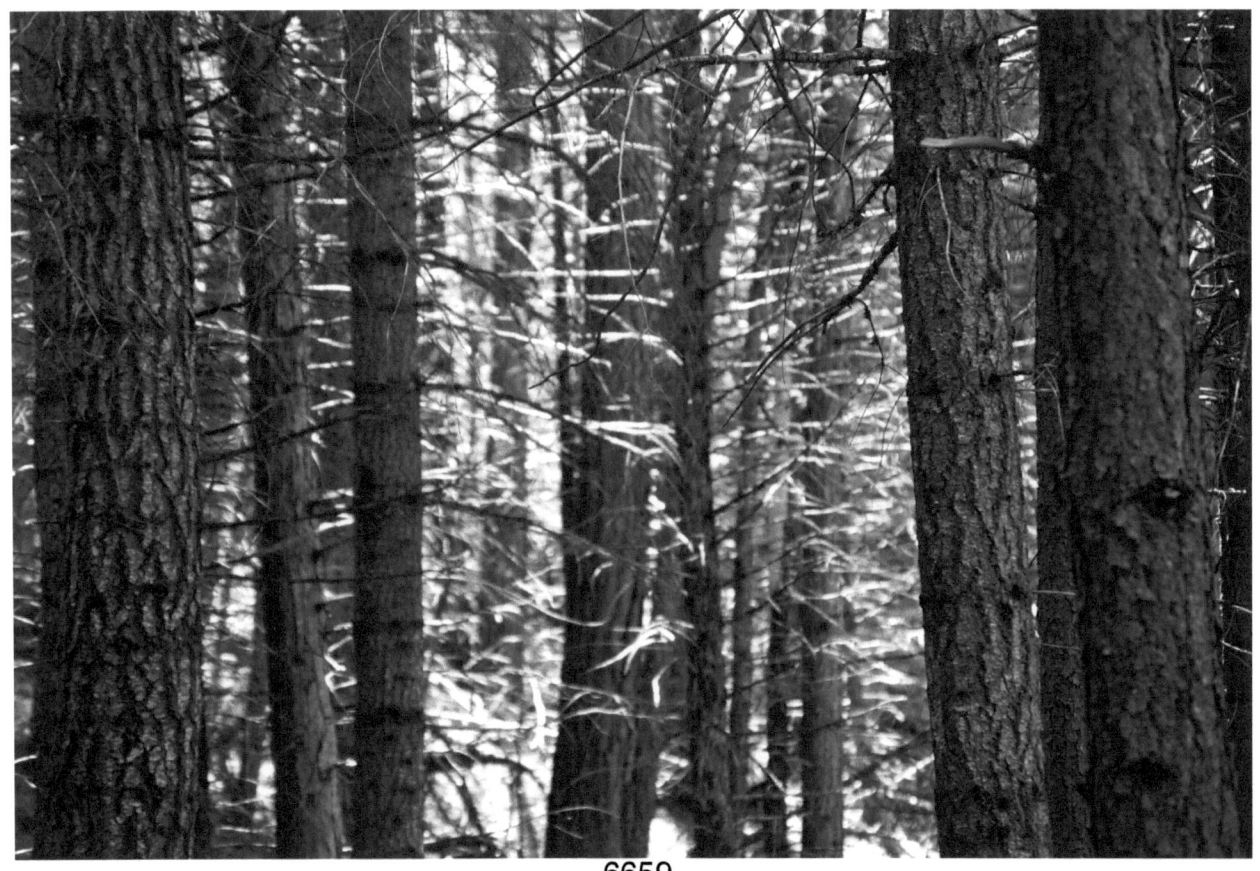
6659

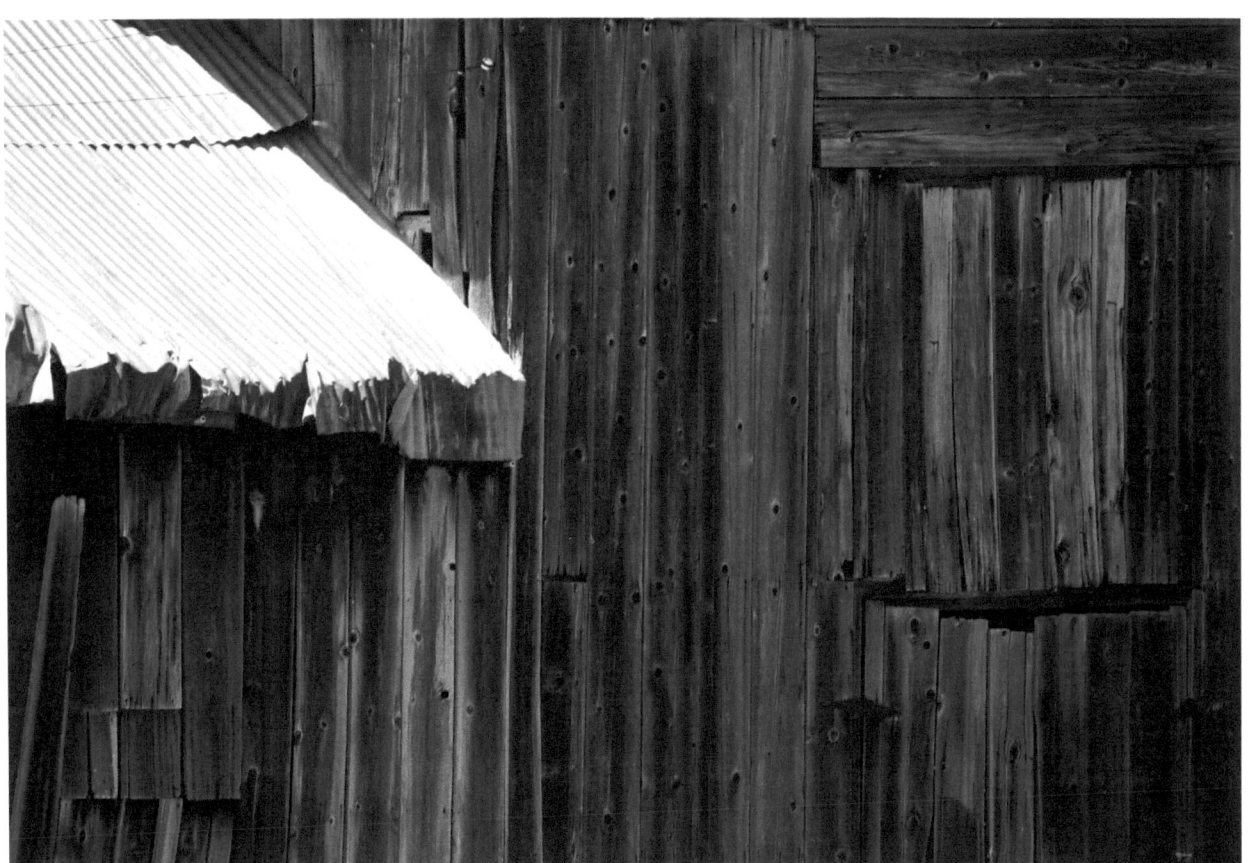
6946

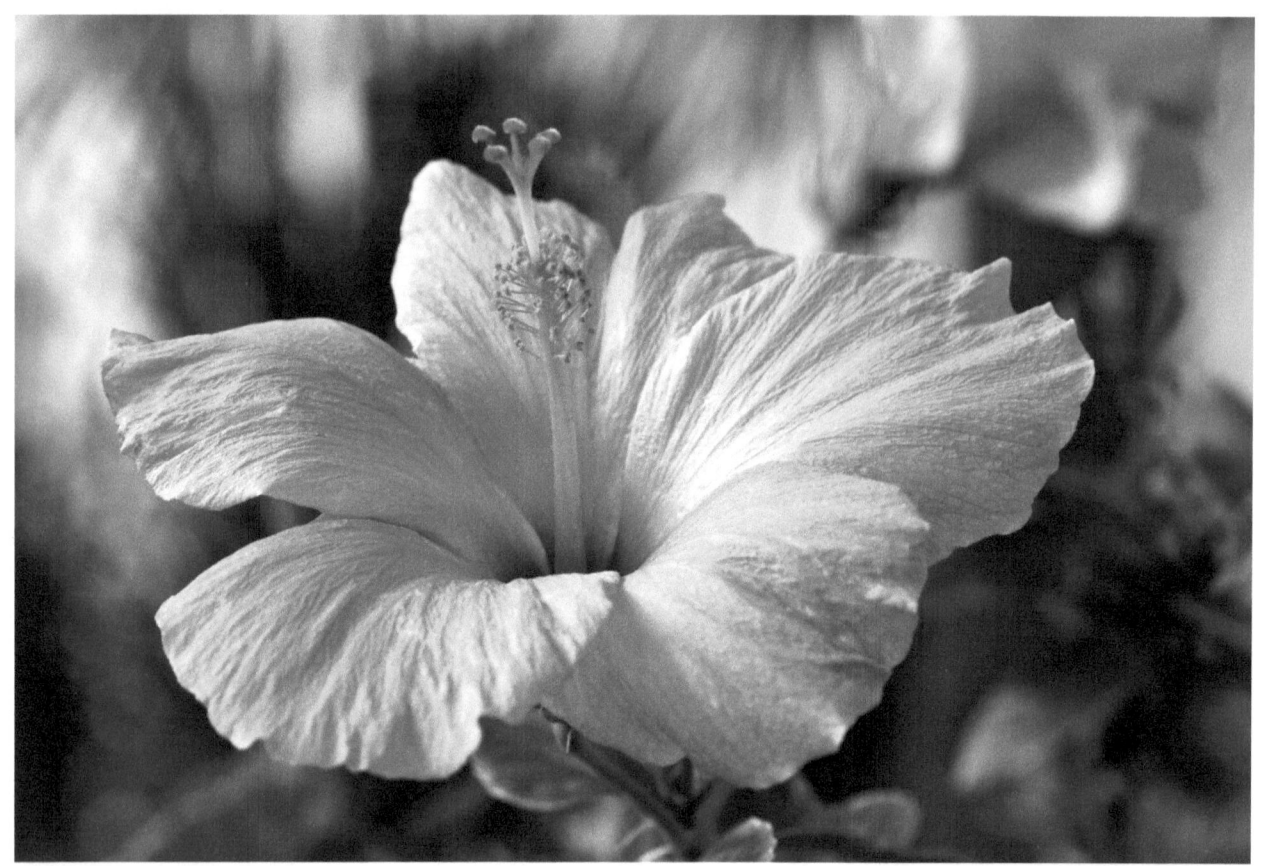

6990

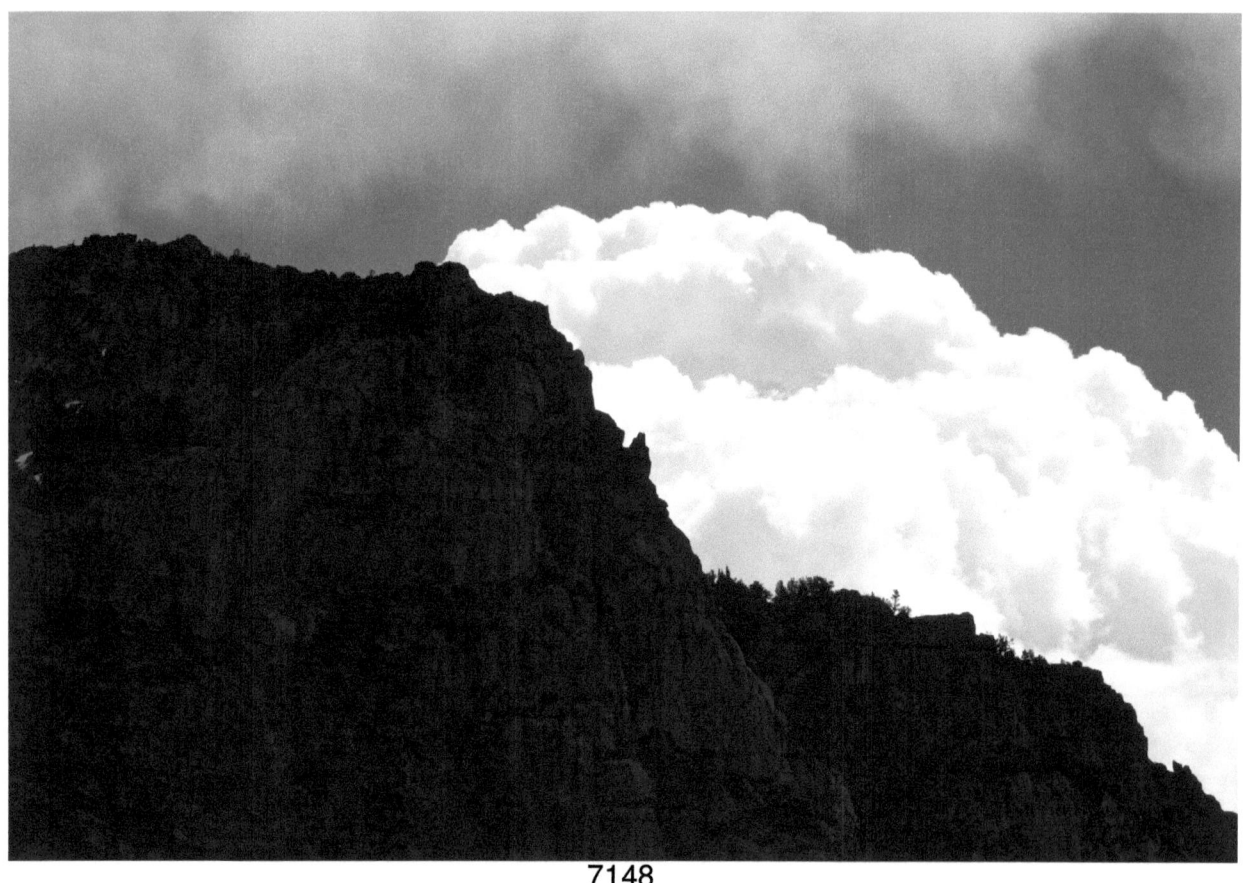

7148

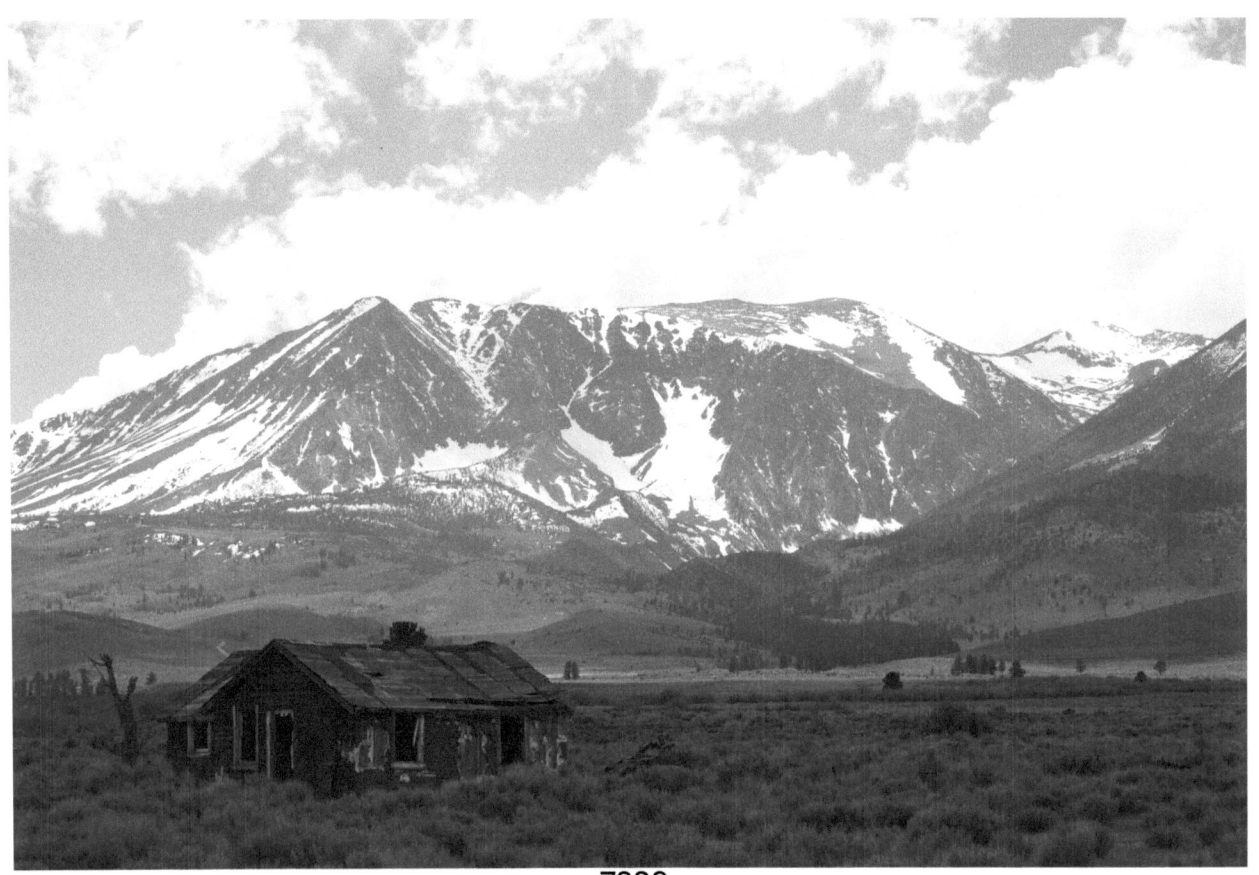

7339

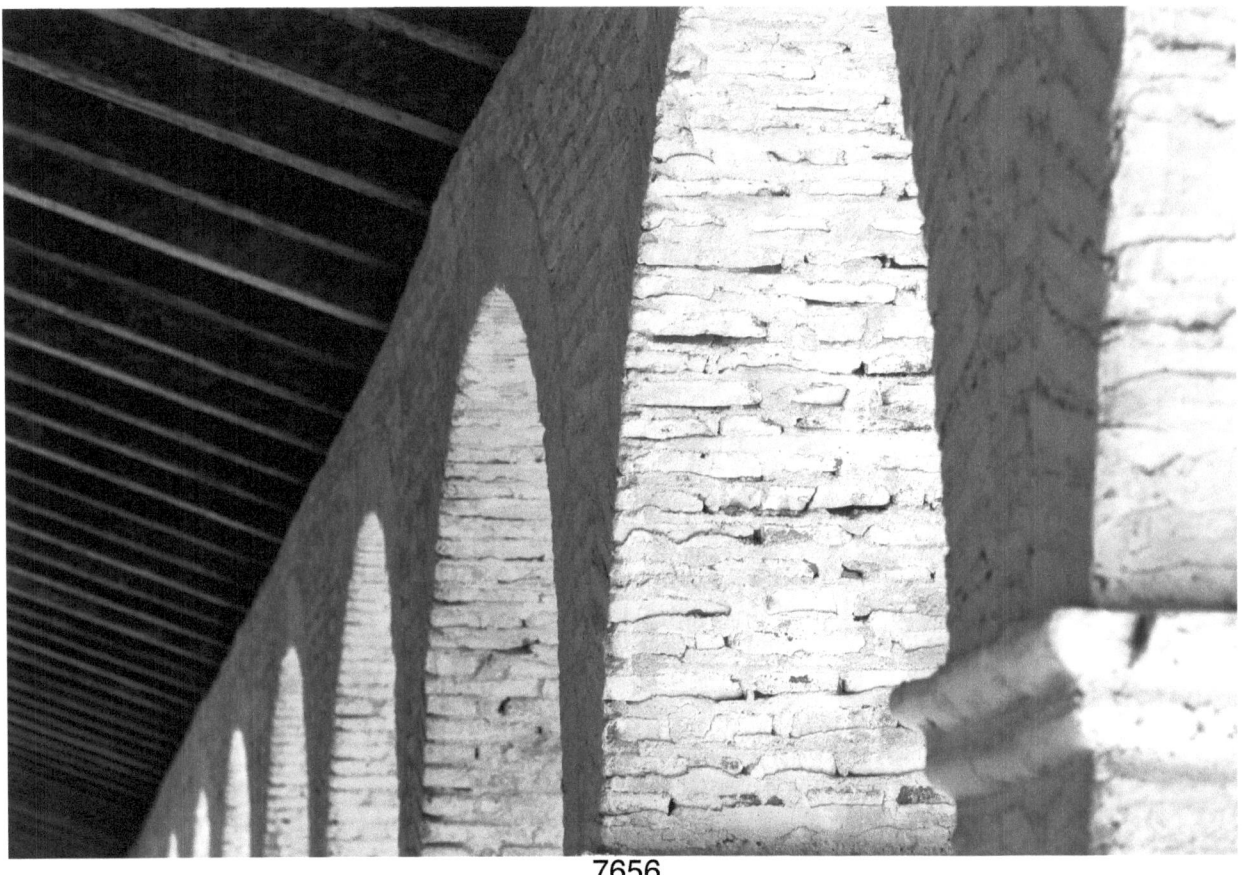

7656

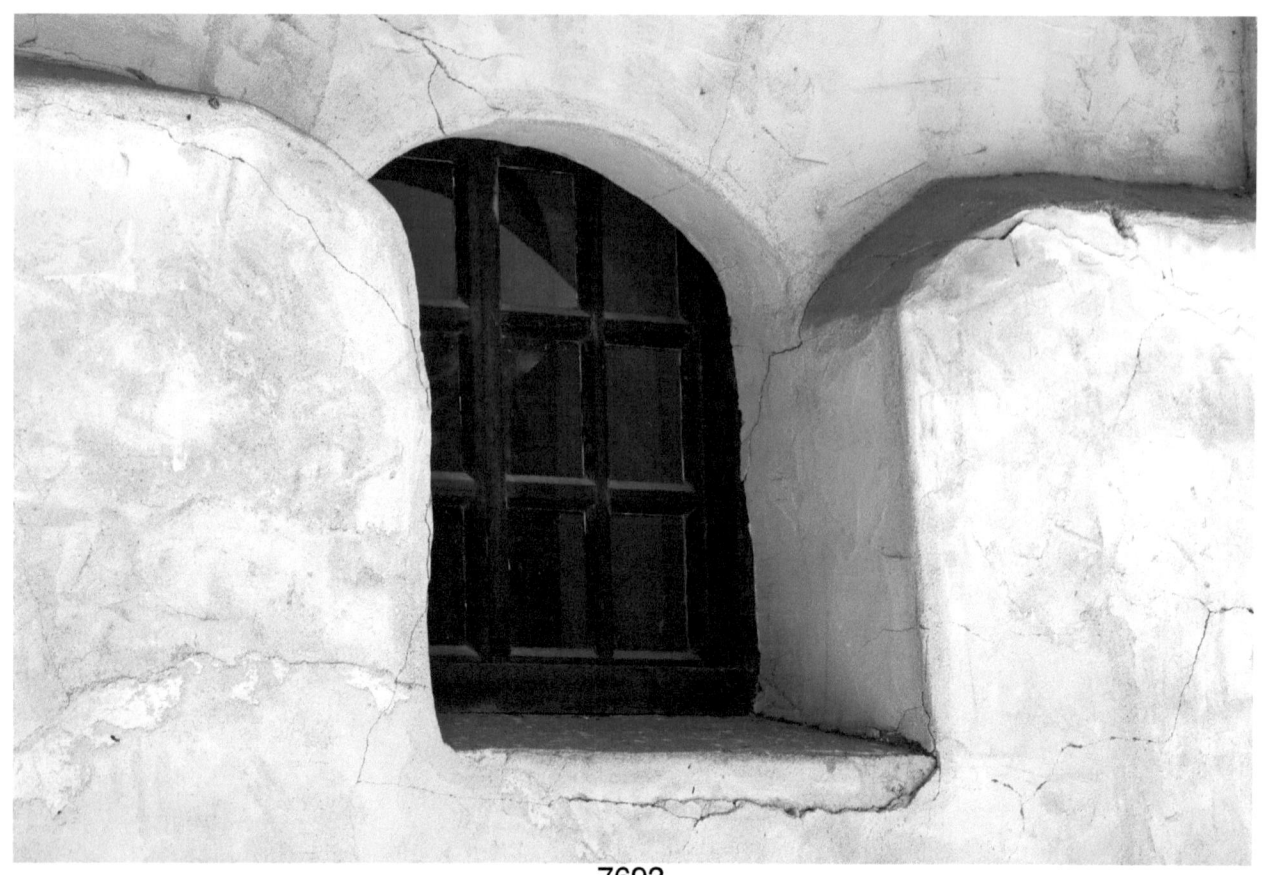

7693

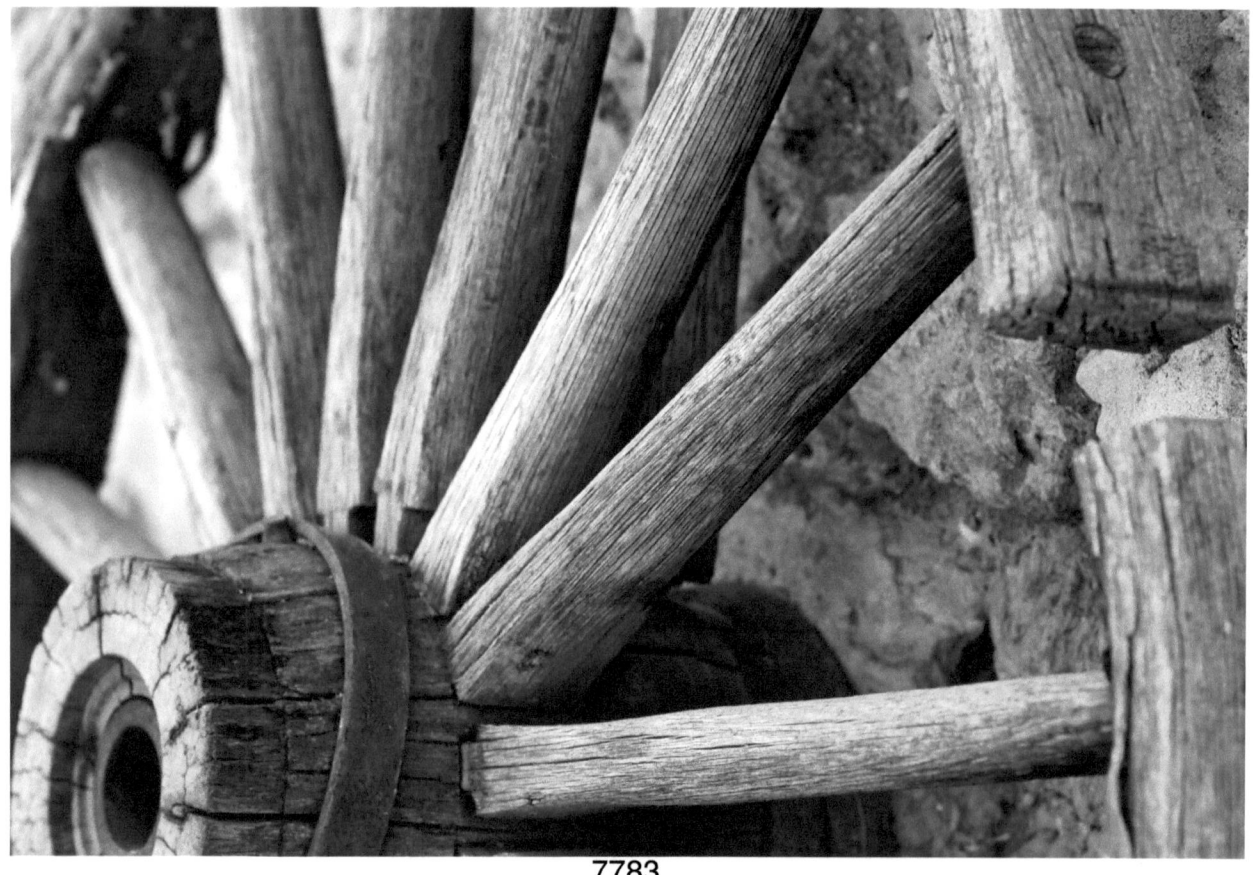

7783

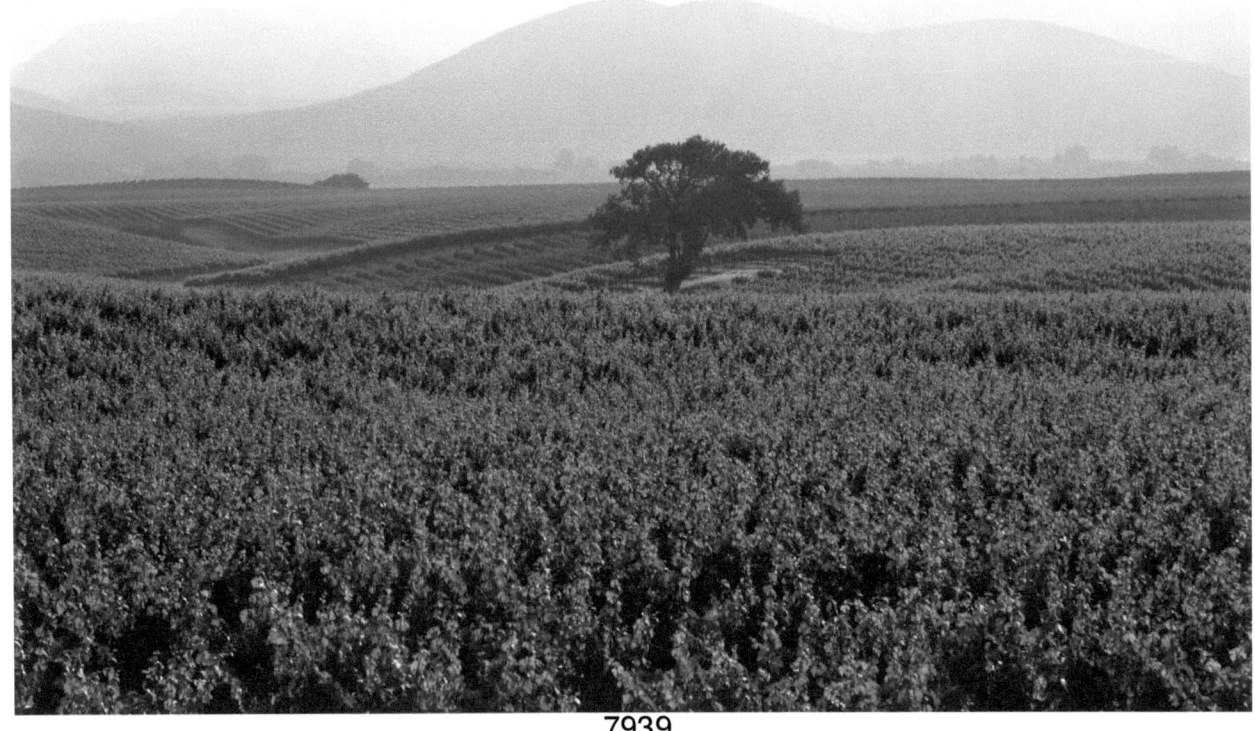

7939

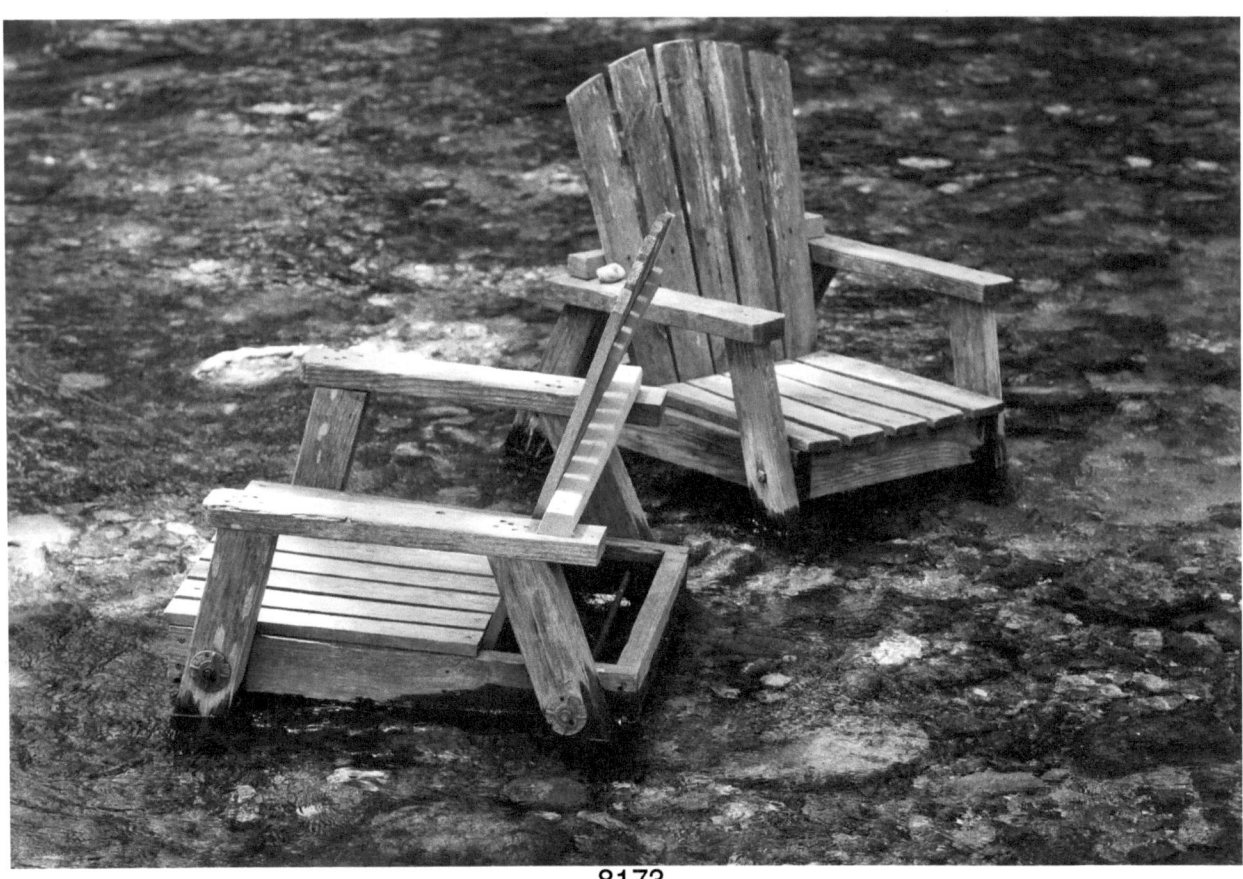

8173

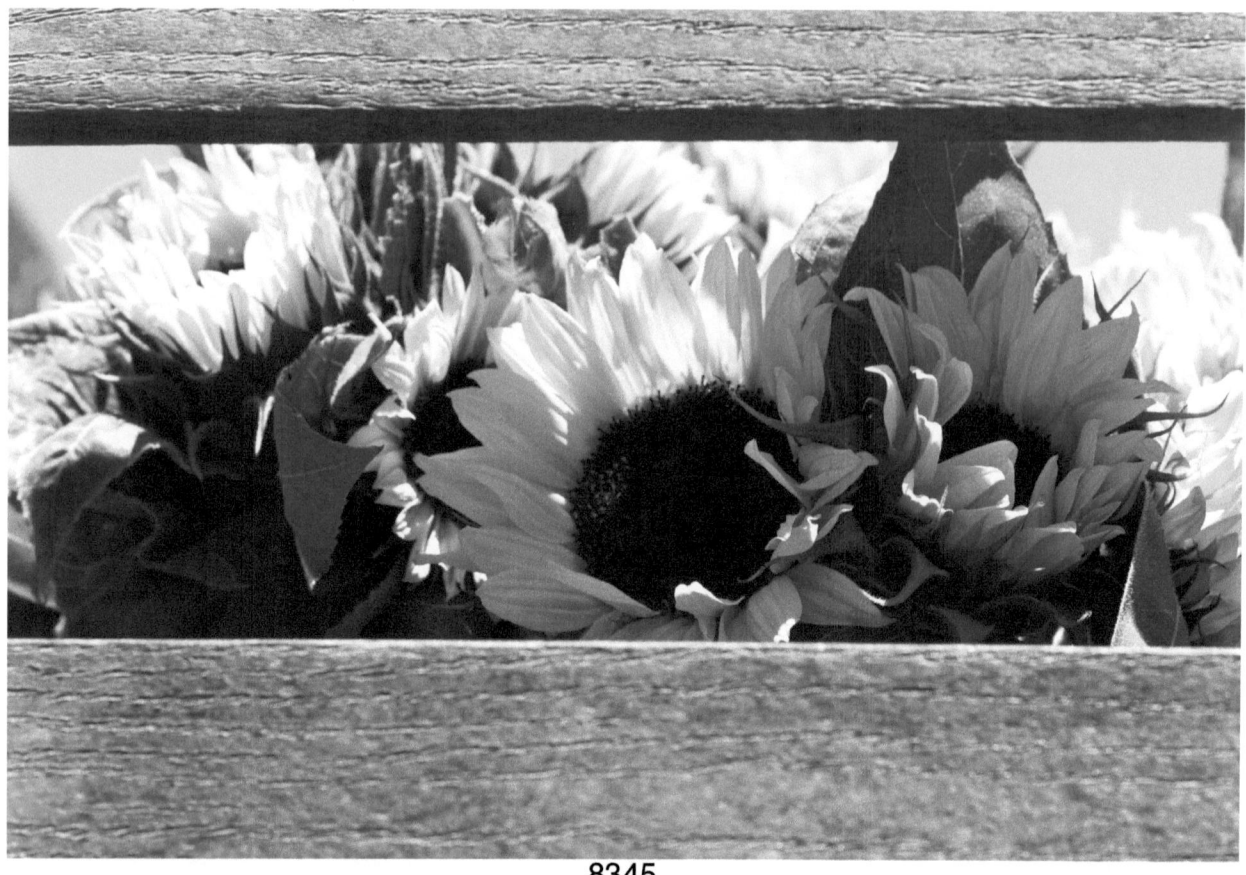

8345

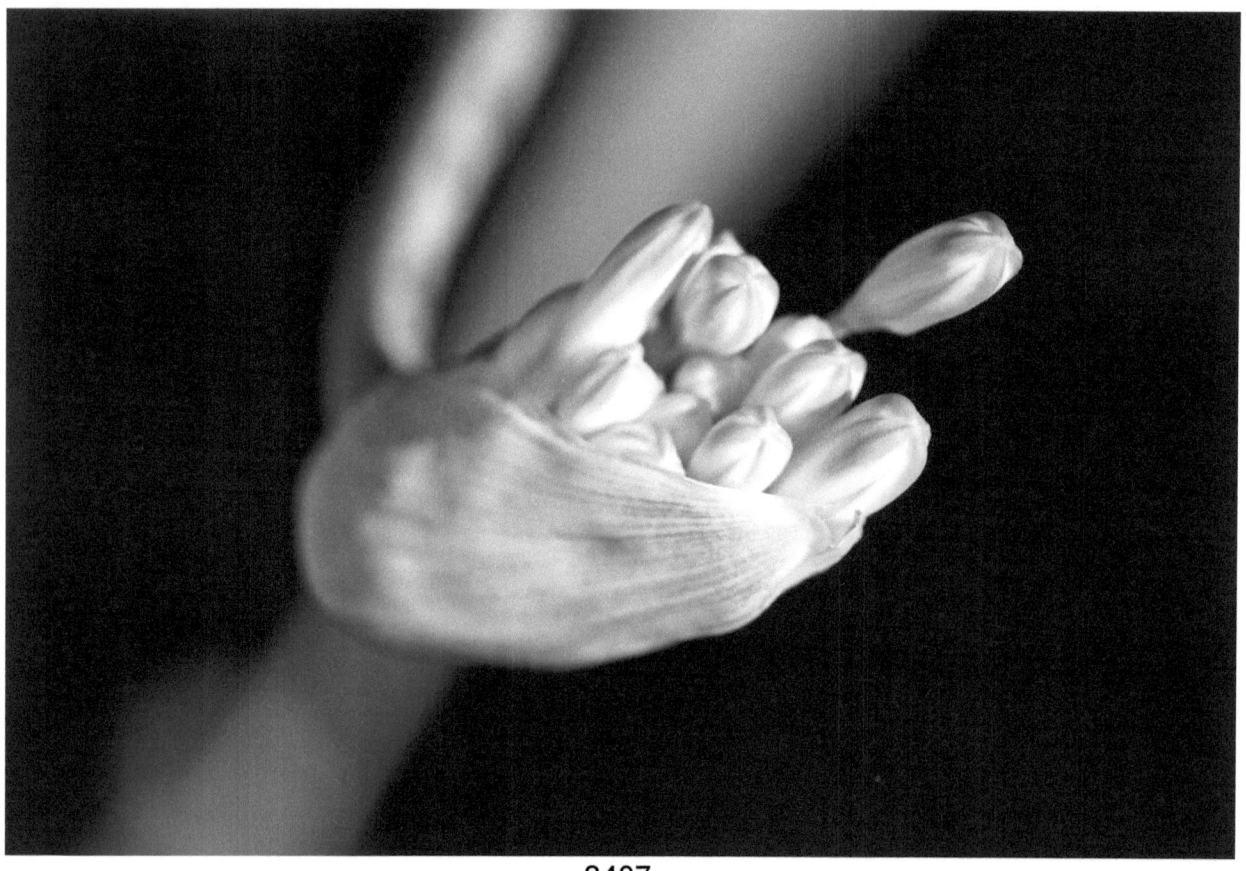

8407

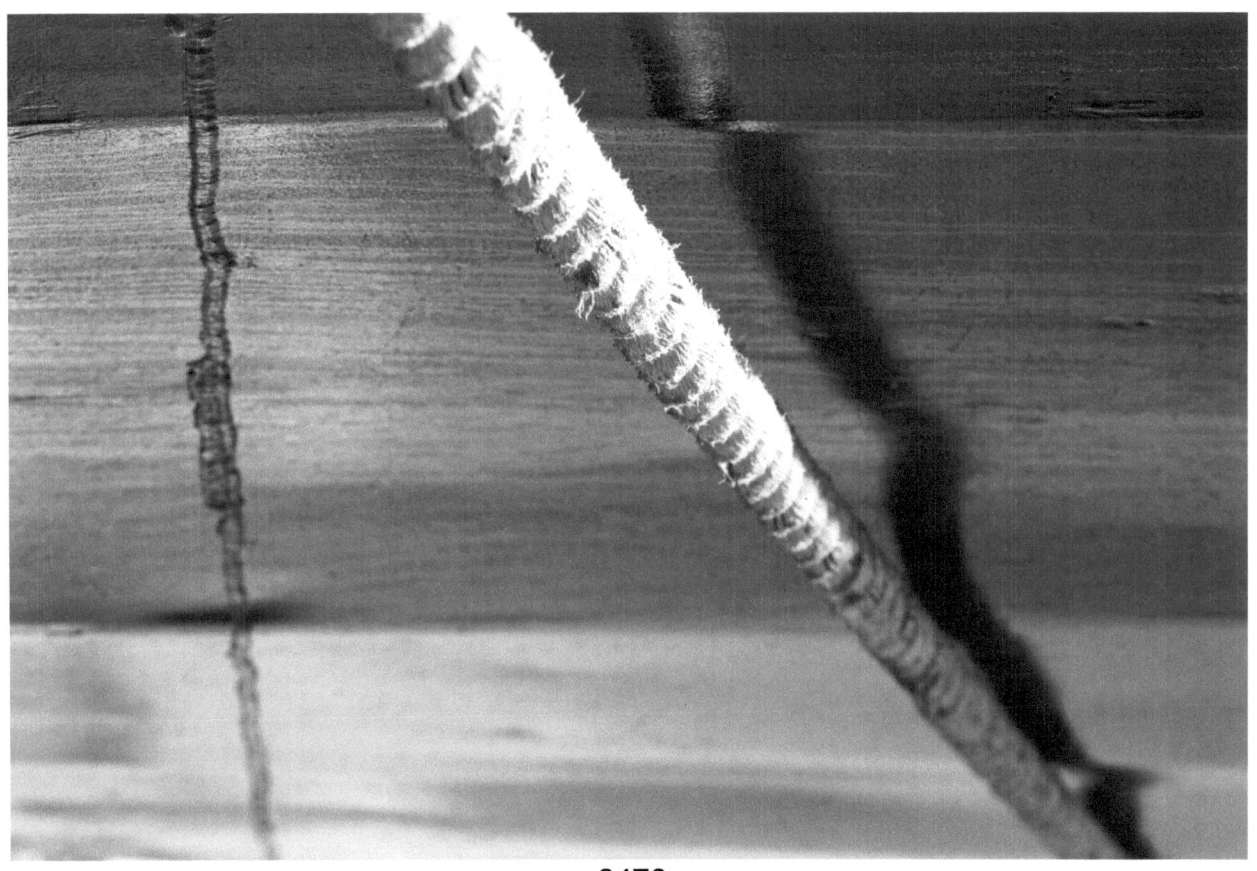

8470

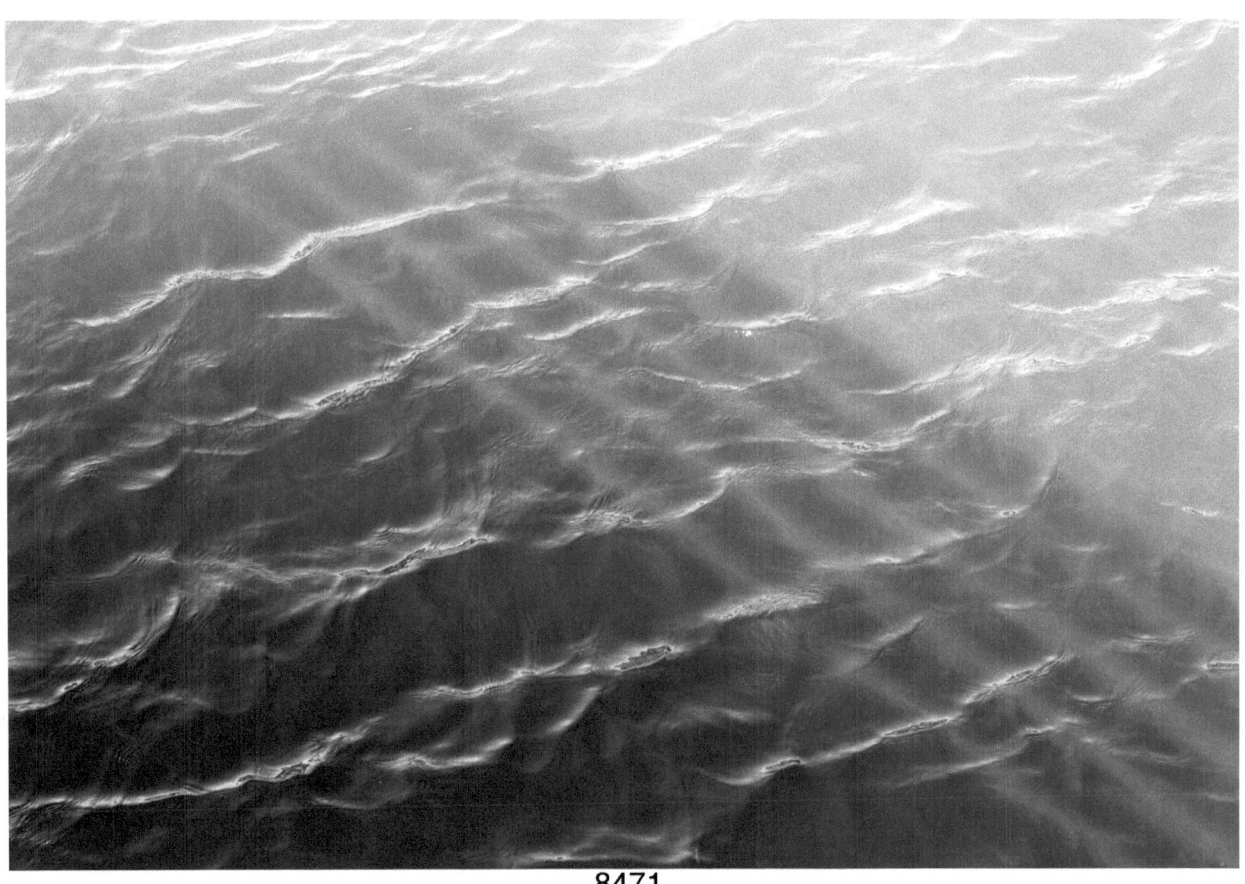

8471

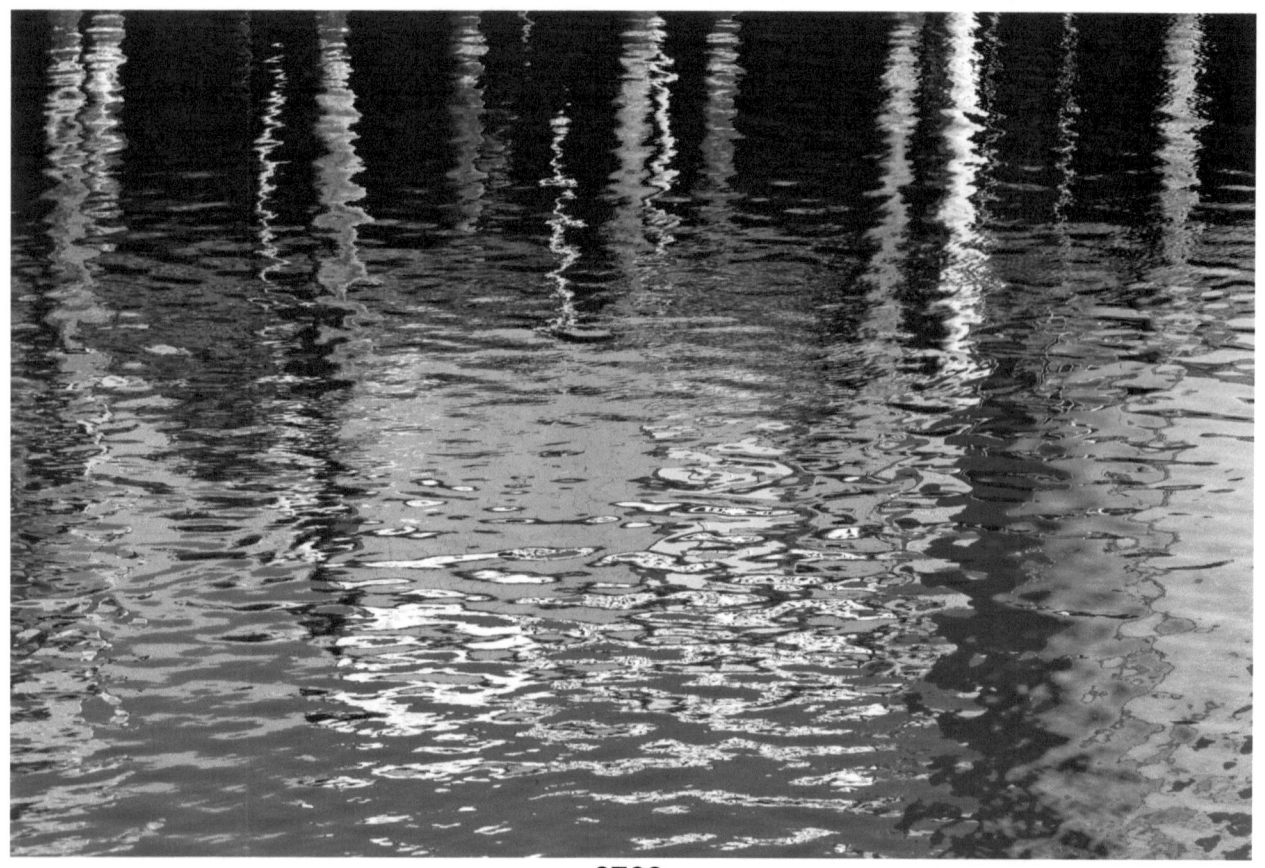

8766

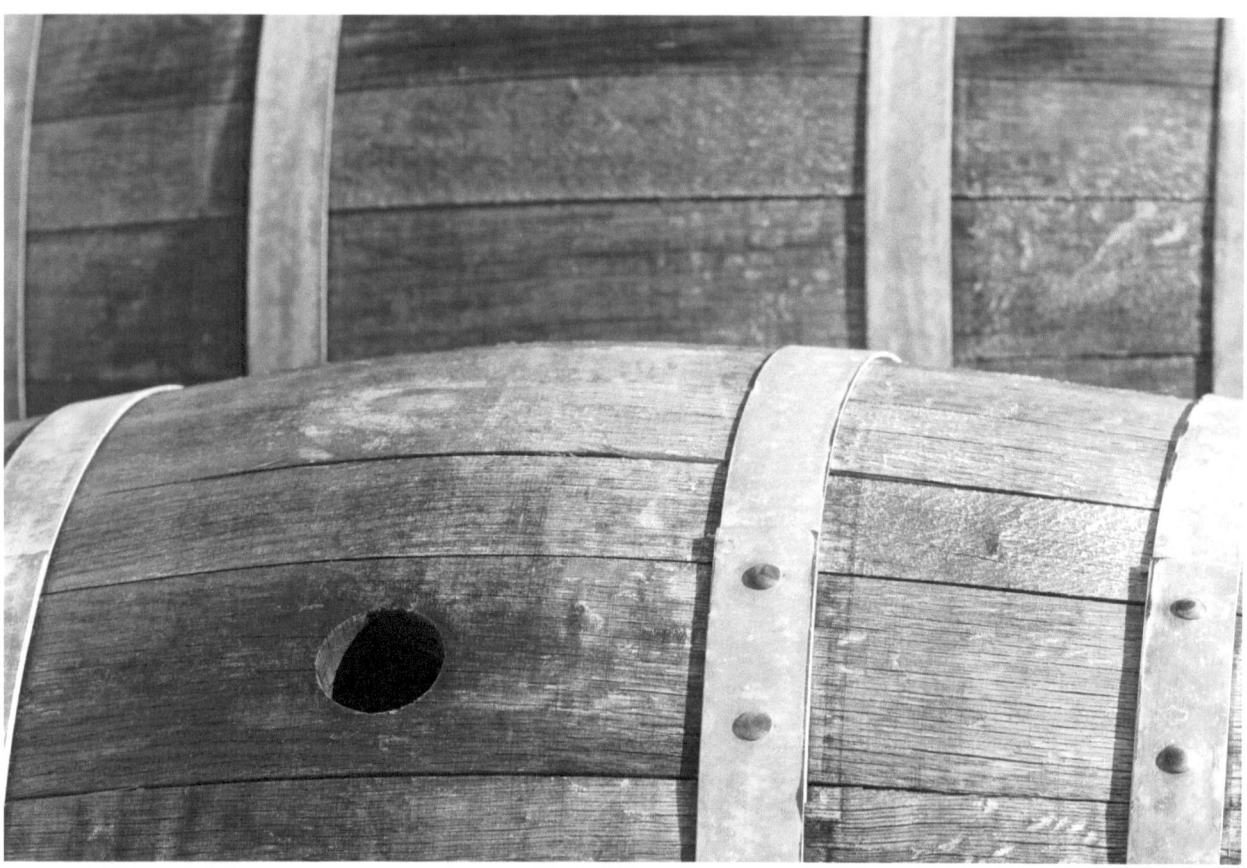

8815

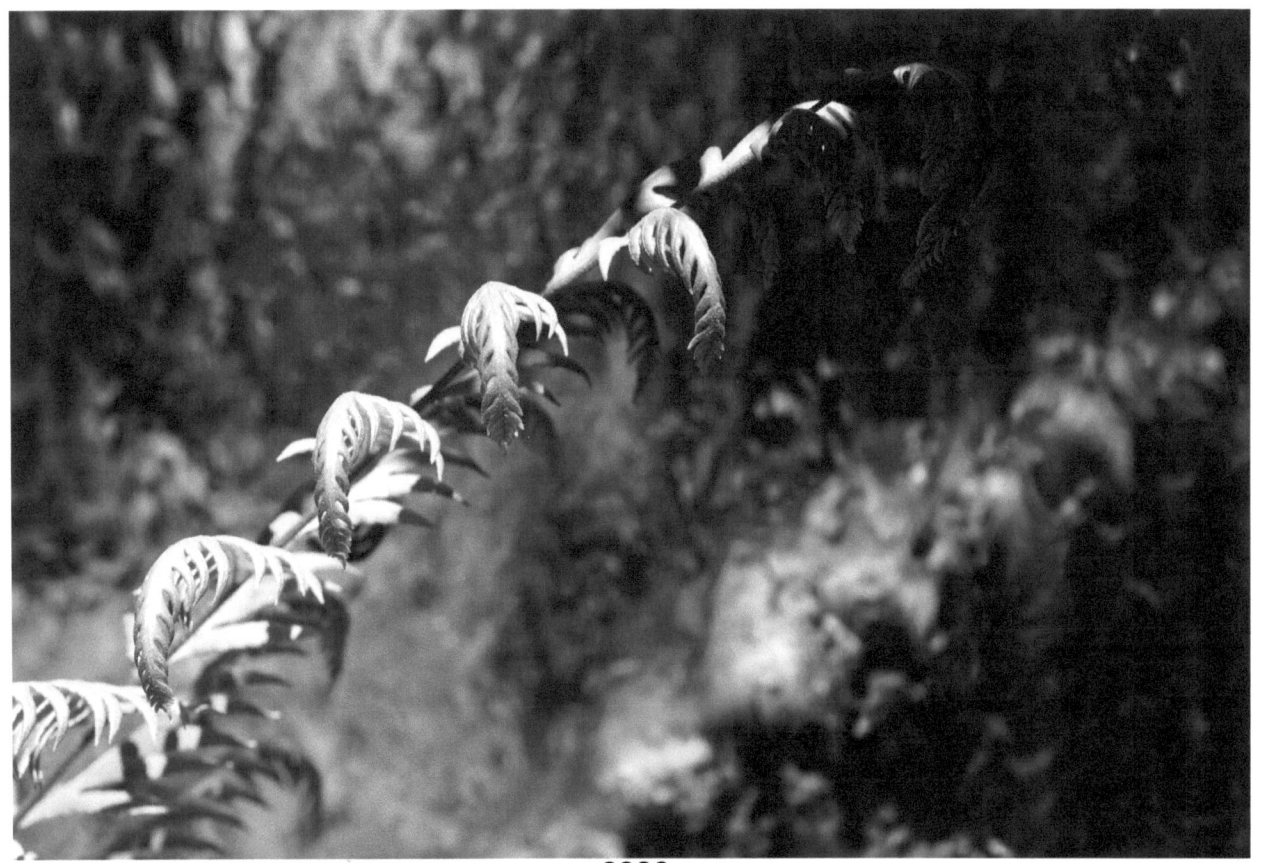

8889

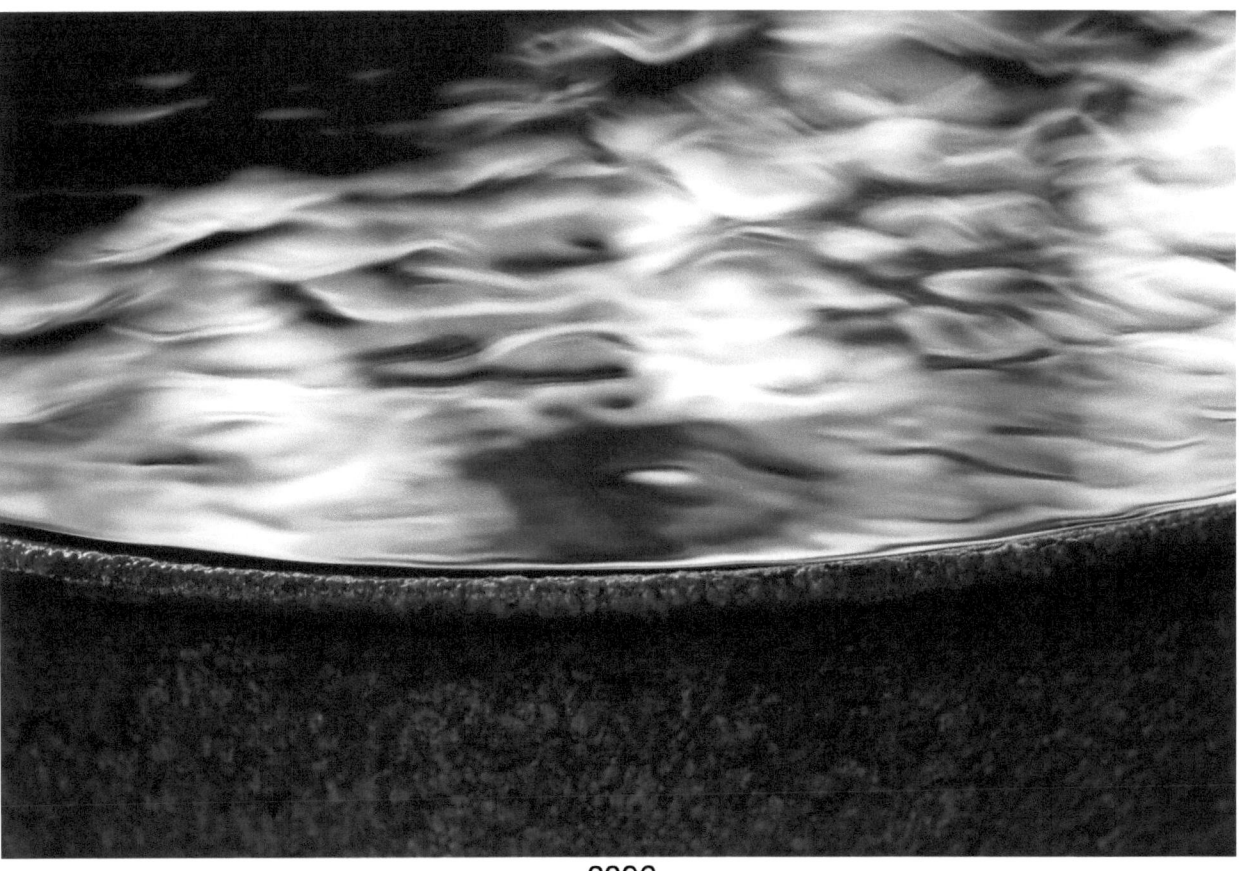

8896

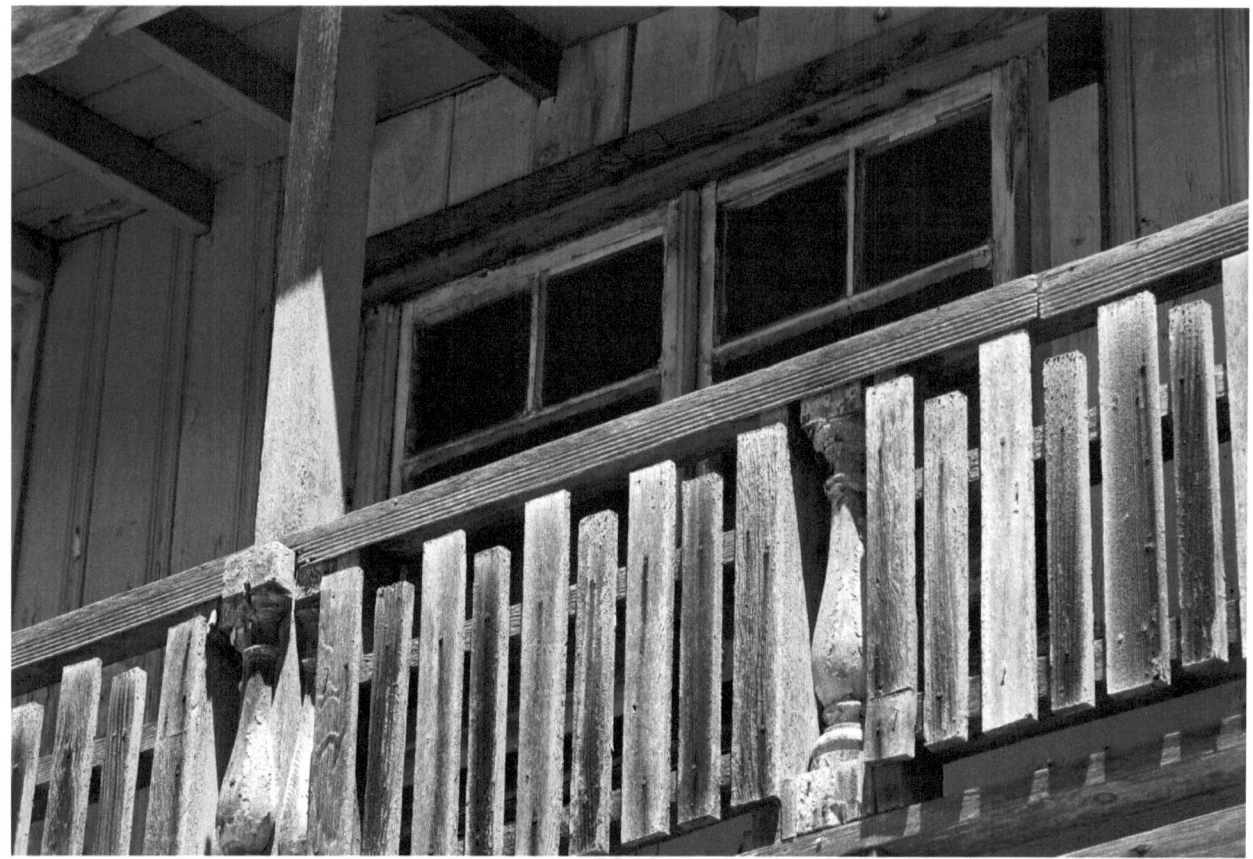

8949

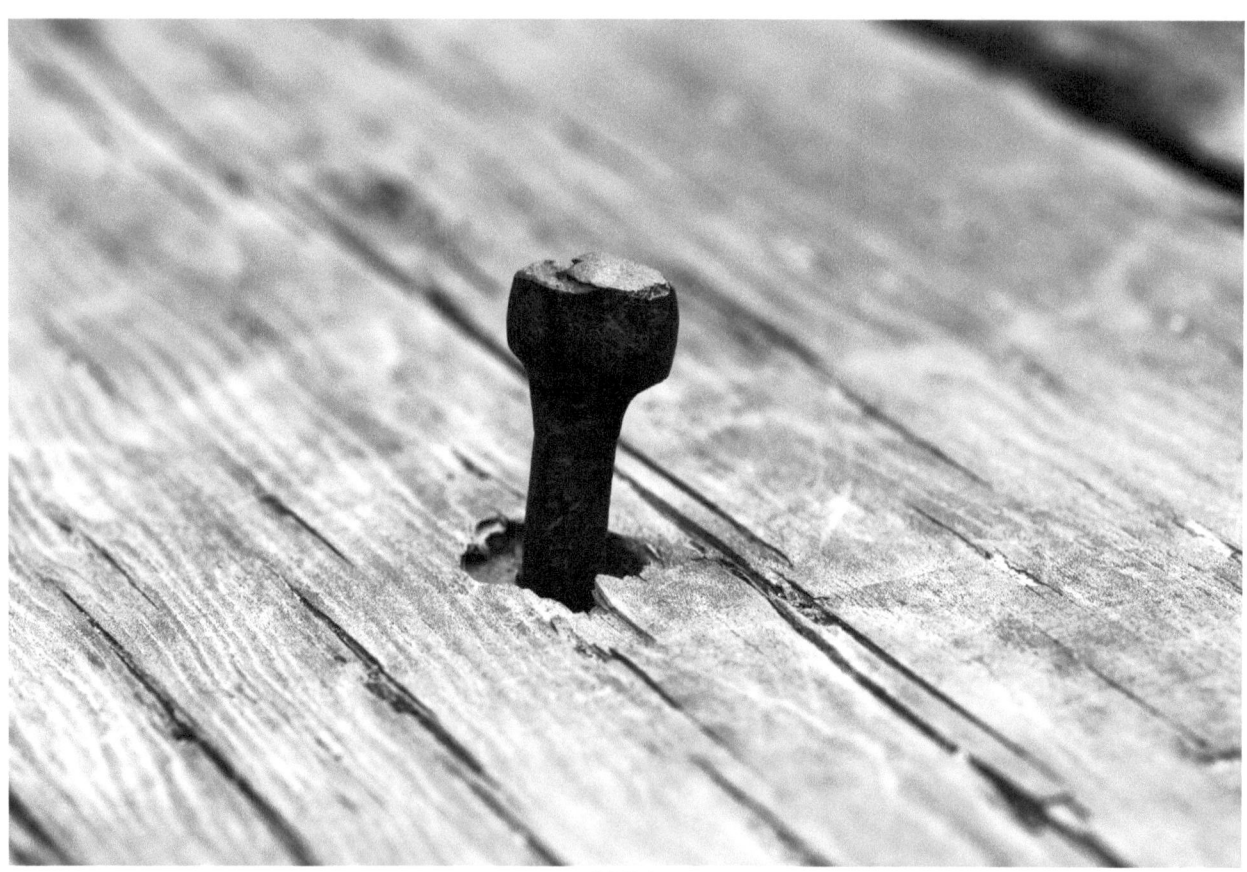

9024

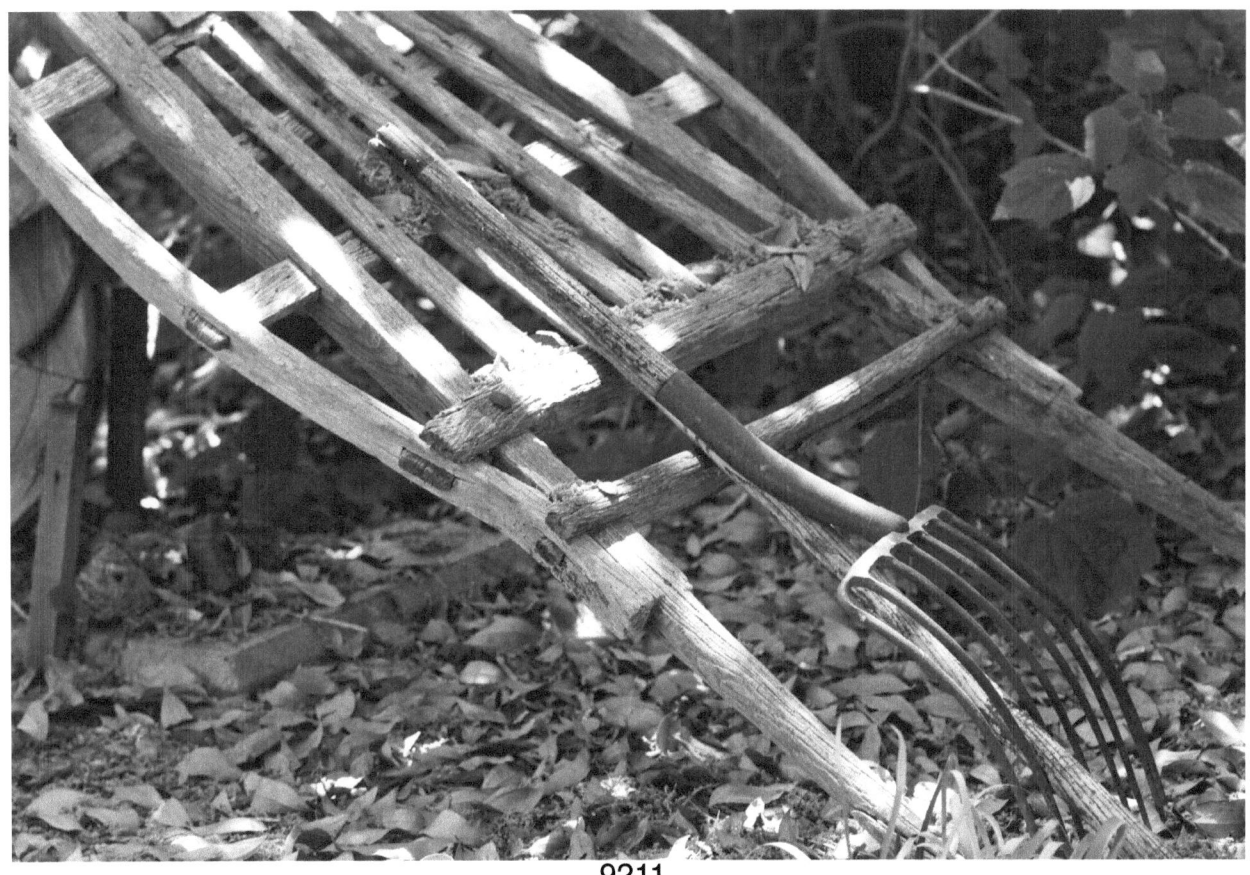

9211

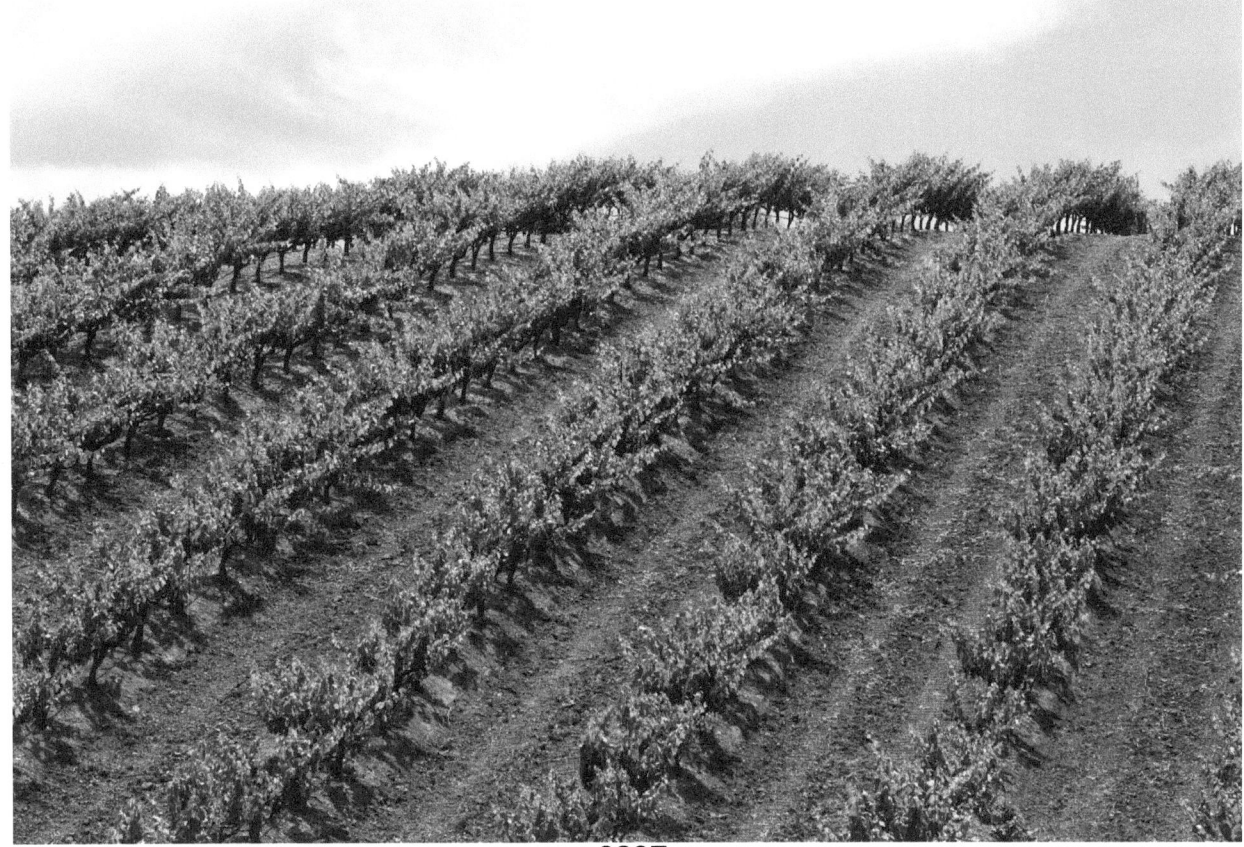

9297

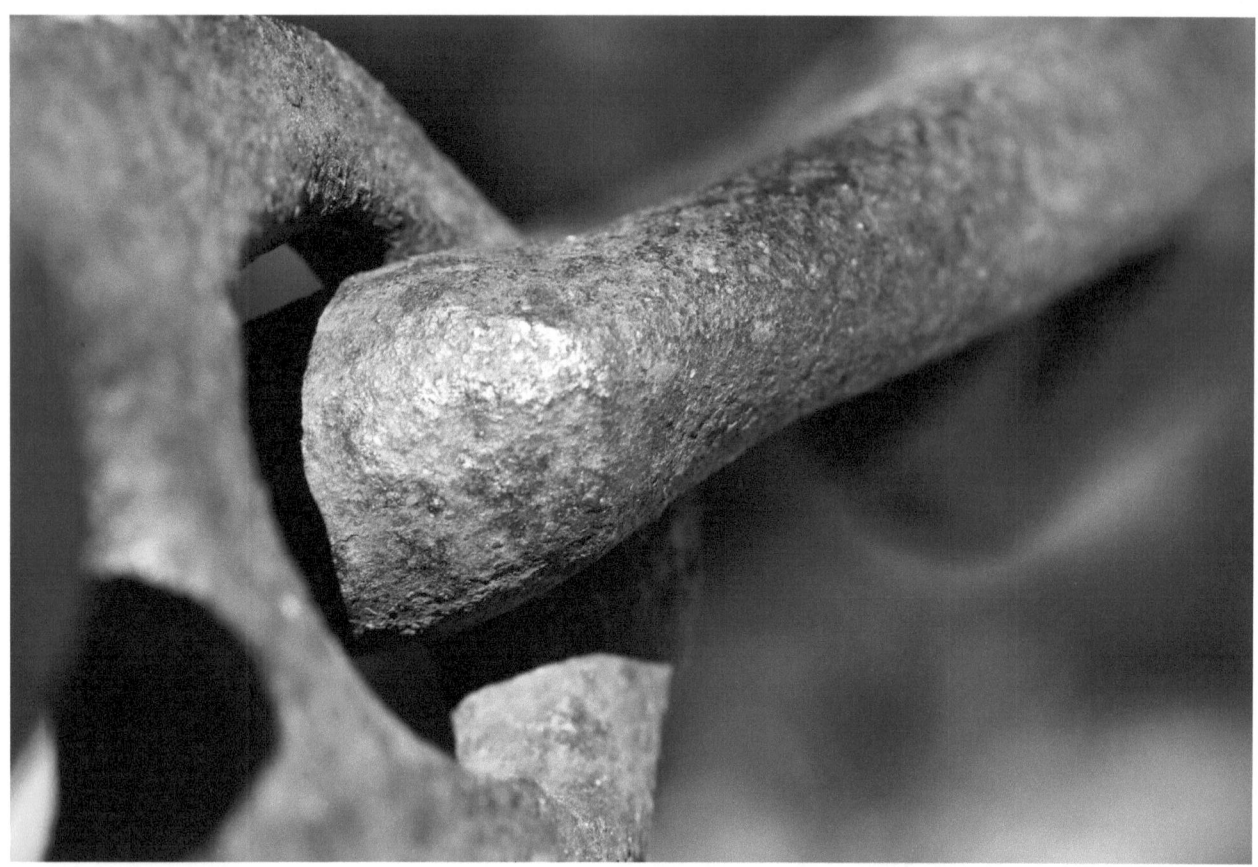

9353

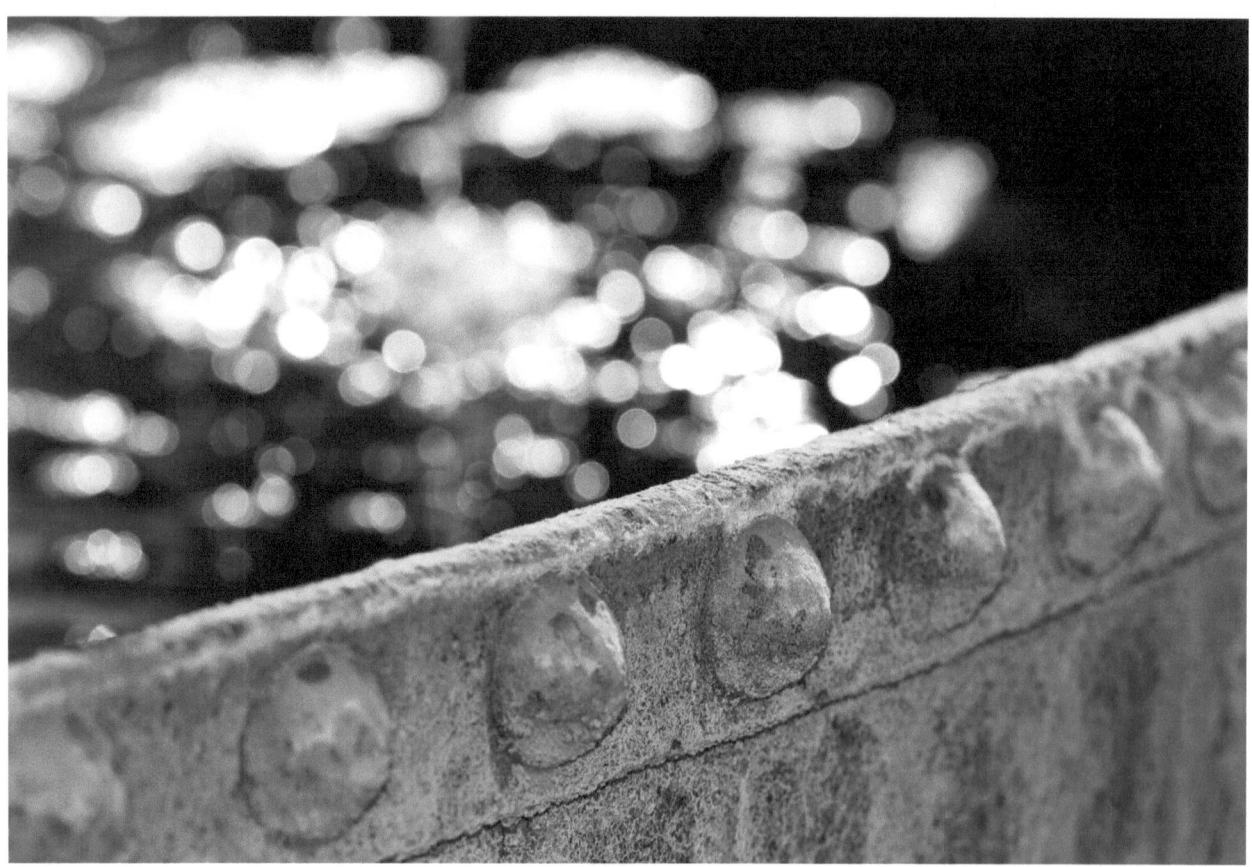

9430

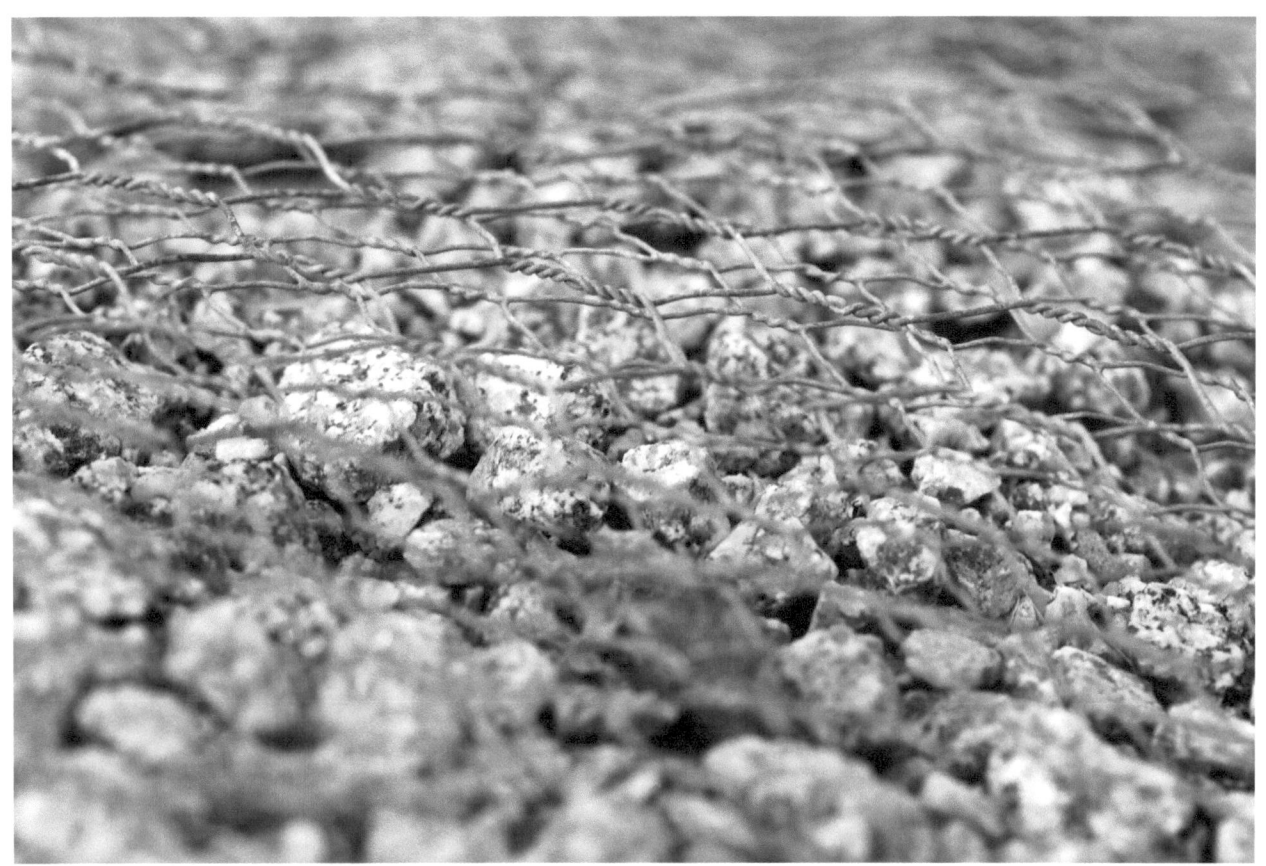

9970

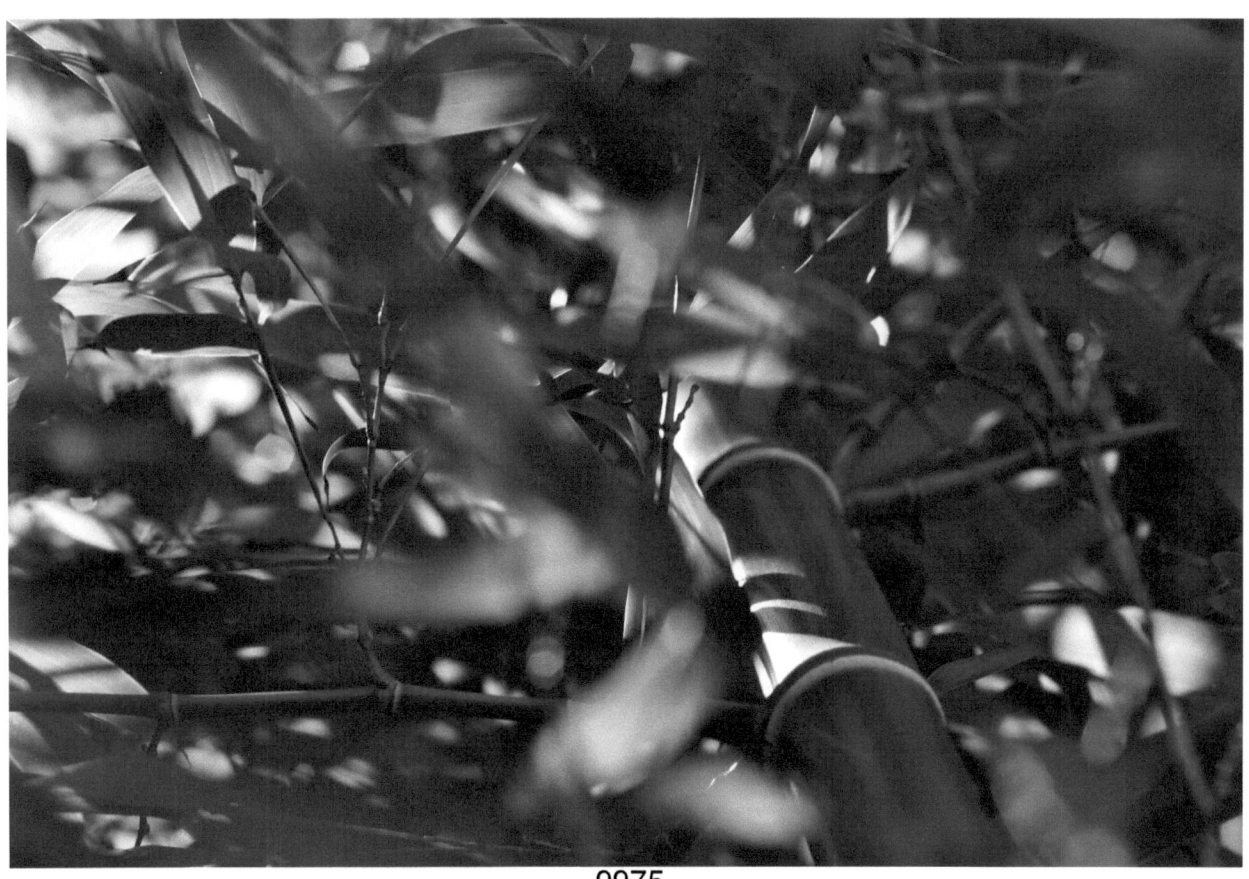

9975

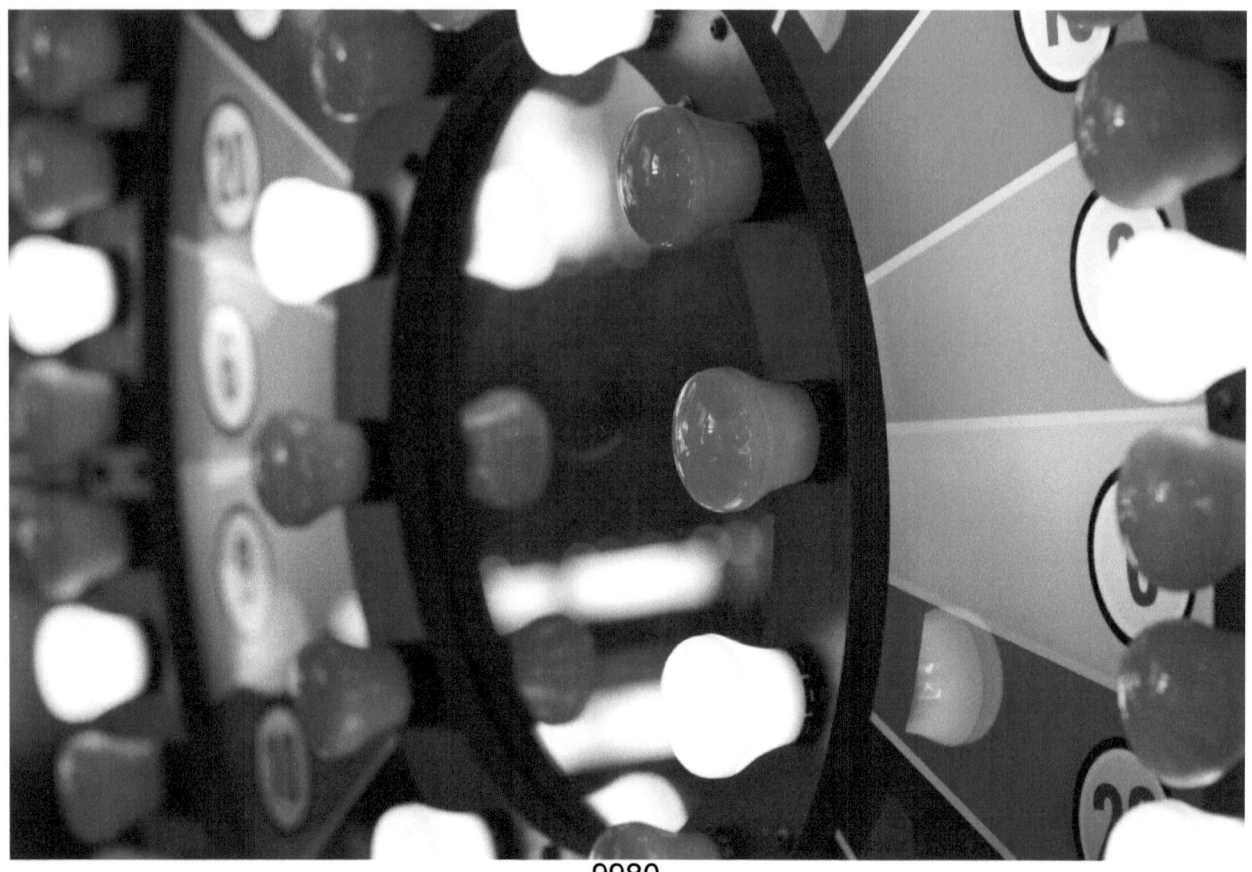

9980

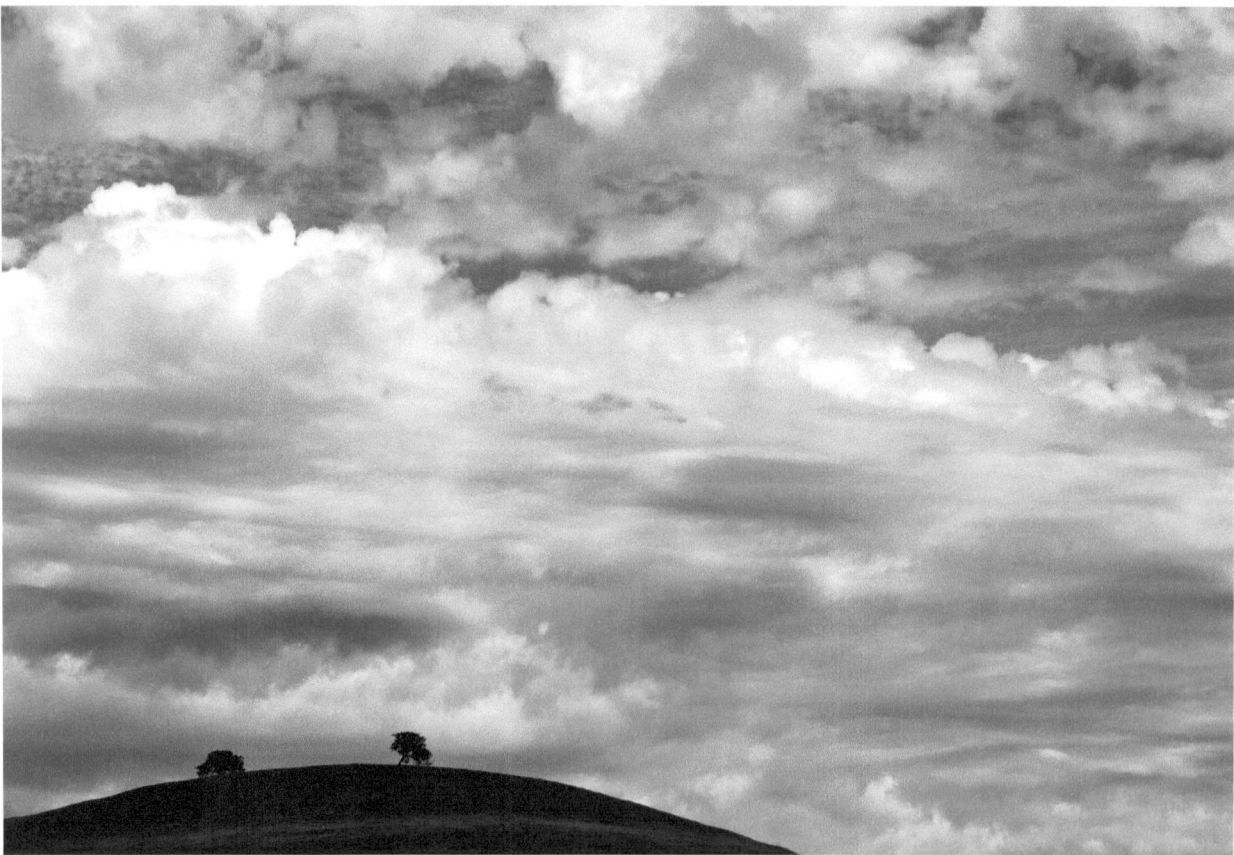

9992

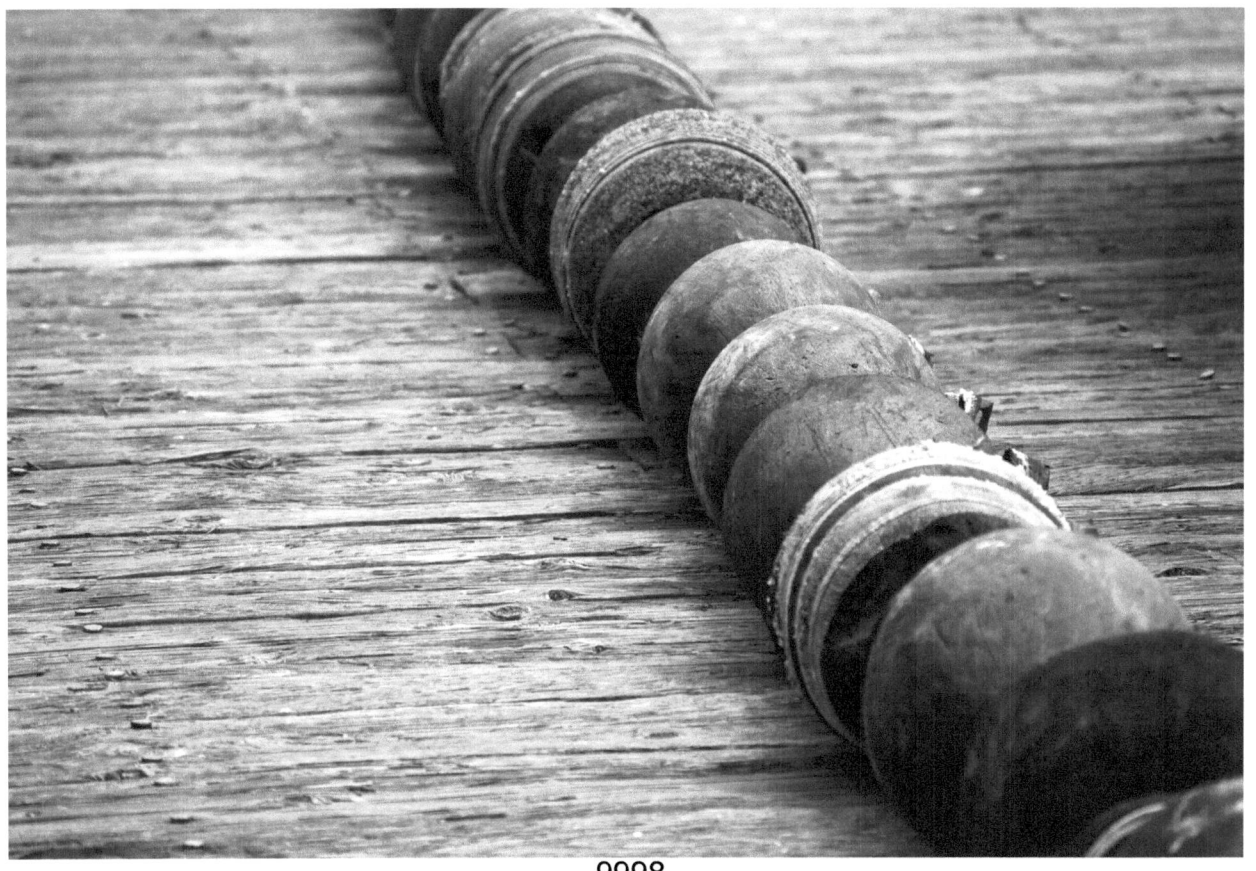

9998

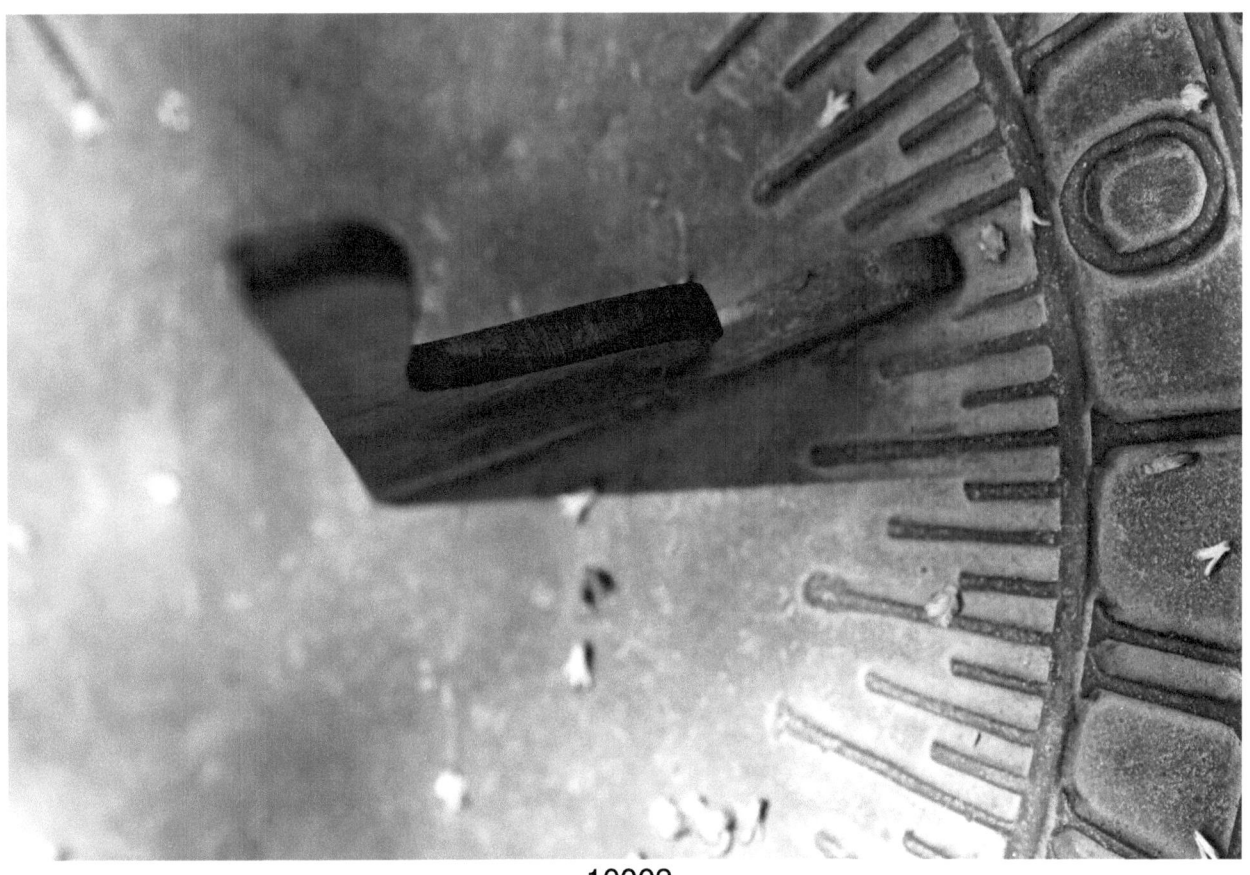

10002